INSTITUTE FOR INTERNATIONAL ECONOMICS

Policy Analyses in International Economics

8

March 1984

AN INTERNATIONAL STANDARD FOR MONETARY STABILIZATION

Ronald I. McKinnon

AN INTERNATIONAL STANDARD FOR MONETARY STABILIZATION

POLICY ANALYSES IN INTERNATIONAL ECONOMICS 8

AN INTERNATIONAL STANDARD FOR MONETARY STABILIZATION

Ronald I. McKinnon

INSTITUTE FOR INTERNATIONAL ECONOMICS
WASHINGTON, DC
MARCH 1984

DISTRIBUTED BY MIT PRESS
CAMBRIDGE, MASSACHUSETTS, AND LONDON, ENGLAND

Ronald I. McKinnon is Eberle Professor of Economics at Stanford University, Stanford, California. He was a Visiting Fellow at the Institute for International Economics during the fall of 1983.

The author wishes to thank the Hoover Institution and the Center for Public Policy Research, Stanford University, for providing additional financial support for this study.

The author would like to thank Kong-Yam Tan of Stanford University for his invaluable econometric and conceptual assistance. Much of the empirical work in chapter 4 parallels that first done in his Stanford Ph.D. dissertation.

Steven Ambler, C. Fred Bergsten, William R. Cline, W. Max Corden, B. S. Cohen, I. M. Destler, Rudiger Dornbusch, Peter B. Kenen, Miguel A. Kiguel, Stephen Marris, Margaret McKinnon, Hans-Eckart Scharrer, Thomas Willet, and John Williamson also provided helpful comments.   R.I. McK.

The Institute for International Economics was created, and is principally funded, by the German Marshall Fund of the United States.

Library of Congress Cataloging in Publication Data

McKinnon, Ronald I.
An international standard for monetary stabilization.

(Policy analyses in international economics ; 7)
1. International finance.   2. Monetary policy.
3. Foreign exchange problem.   I. Institute for International Economics
(U.S.)   II. Title.   III. Series.
Bibliography: p. 95
HG3881.M395 1984   332.4'56   83-22572
ISBN 0-88132-018-8
ISBN 0-262-63093-1 (MIT Press)

Contents

TEXT FIGURES

Preface

Over the past dozen years, the world economy has been wracked by rampant inflation, deep recession, recurrent exchange rate misalignment among major currencies, and increasing trade restrictions. In this study, Ronald I. McKinnon suggests a common cause for many of these ills: the narrowly *national* orientation of monetary policies in a world where markets for goods and capital have become increasingly *international*. The consequence is endemic financial imbalance in the world economy.

In particular, McKinnon argues that the asymmetrical position of the dollar in world finance and the absence of monetary policy coordination among the major countries resulted in the two great inflations of the 1970s and the sharp recession of the early 1980s. However, he believes there is a way out of this instability and makes a set of innovative proposals for doing so.

In each industrial country, McKinnon argues that the central bank should deemphasize purely national monetary indicators, such as interest rates or growth in domestic money, and increase the weight assigned to stabilizing the exchange rate against a hard currency trading partner. Such an outward-looking monetary policy need not conflict with domestic macroeconomic goals: he argues that the exchange rate is a robust leading indicator of changes needed in the nation's money supply to prevent unexpected inflation or deflation.

To stabilize the world economy, however, more is required of the major monetary authorities—in particular, the US Federal Reserve System and the central banks of Germany and Japan. In addition to smoothing fluctuations in the yen/dollar and mark/dollar exchange rates, they also need to cooperate to stabilize the absolute purchasing power of their currencies. Proper joint control over their *aggregate* money stock would then dampen (and even avoid) worldwide economic cycles of boom and bust.

As background for these proposals, the introduction to the study describes the evolution of the international monetary system from the late 1940s to the 1980s and argues that monetary control was lost in the early 1970s with the shift from fixed to floating exchange rates. Impatient readers can skip to chapter 5 for the details of how a new international monetary standard could be constructed—with explicit coordination among the Federal Reserve System, the Bundesbank, and the Bank of Japan. Because of changed circumstances, this new system would be quite different from the regime created at Bretton Woods in 1944.

The intervening chapters are important for understanding McKinnon's case for a new international monetary standard. Chapter 2 suggests that previously persuasive arguments in favor of floating exchange rates are either incorrect or have become obsolete. Chapter 3 argues that any country, acting in its own best interests, should gear domestic monetary policy toward stabilizing its nominal exchange rate with some major hard currency trading partner(s).

Most importantly, chapter 4 provides empirical evidence that the United States—the center country—can no longer successfully conduct an autonomous monetary policy. The Federal Reserve, McKinnon argues, cannot afford to ignore the impact of international capital movements on the American monetary system and, through the exchange rate, on the American economy. Money growth in other hard currency countries affects the American economy now much more than it did in the 1950s and 1960s.

Many observers of international economic affairs will be aware that McKinnon has presented some of these ideas in previous writings. This new study, however, is different in several respects. First, it pulls together all components of McKinnon's analysis into a single, concise treatise. Second, it responds to several criticisms of his earlier work (in particular, with regard to the concept of "indirect currency substitution" now presented in chapter 3). Third, it offers a substantial amount of new empirical support for McKinnon's thesis. Fourth, and perhaps most important, it suggests a much more evolutionary—and thus presumably more practical—set of proposals for putting in place the policy reforms that McKinnon believes would bring stability to the American and world economies.

This is the first time that the Institute for International Economics has published a study not by a member of its own staff—although much of the paper was prepared while Professor McKinnon was a Visiting Fellow at the Institute in the fall of 1983. We do so because we believe the ideas presented here are of considerable importance in both understanding the international economic events of the past decade or so and in charting a course toward greater stability in the future. We hope that this publication will increase the attention paid to McKinnon's innovative and provocative approach, particularly in official circles throughout the world.

The Institute for International Economics is a private nonprofit research institution for the study and discussion of international economic policy. Its purpose is to analyze important issues in that area, and to develop and communicate practical new approaches for dealing with them.

The Institute was created in November 1981 through a generous commitment of funds from the German Marshall Fund of the United States. Financial support has been received from other private foundations and corporations, including a grant from the United States–Japan Foundation for partial support of this study. The Institute is completely nonpartisan.

The Board of Directors bears overall responsibility for the Institute and gives general guidance and approval to its research program—including identification of topics that are likely to become important to international economic policymakers over the period of, generally, one to three years. The Director of the Institute, working closely with the staff and outside Advisory Committee, is responsible for the development of particular projects and makes the final decision to publish an individual study.

The Institute hopes that its studies and other activities will contribute to building a stronger foundation for international economic policy around the world. Comments as to how it can best do so are invited from readers of these publications.

C. FRED BERGSTEN
Director

1 Introduction: The Evolving World Dollar Standard

Everybody understands that Western industrial economies have become more open to foreign trade in the last 35 years. International competition is increasingly pervasive—indeed sometimes overwhelming—in national markets for manufactured goods. Since 1948, the General Agreement on Tariffs and Trade (GATT) has, until recently, successfully lessened official interventions—tariffs, quotas, and subsidies—in foreign trade among industrial countries. To be sure, important exceptions abound, and the threat of backsliding on the GATT is all too real in today's unstable financial environment. Nevertheless, commercial rules governing international trade in minerals and most manufactures, and in some services, are substantially the same as those prevailing within individual industrial economies. (The GATT has been much less successful in promoting free trade in agricultural products, which were excluded from the agreement early on at the behest of the United States.)

In contrast to freer trade in goods, the freer flow of private portfolio capital has come about almost inadvertently. With memories of "hot" money flows from the 1920s and 1930s, the 1944 Bretton Woods Agreements envisioned tight exchange controls over private capital movements in the postwar economic order. Article VIII confined the obligation to achieve currency "convertibility" to current account transactions. Article VI specifically prohibited use of resources of the International Monetary Fund (IMF) to finance outflows of private capital. "While wartime planning for the postwar order envisaged an open multilateral trading system, there was no similar intention to restore an open international capital market" (Williamson 1983, p. 7).

Nevertheless, the unplanned evolution of the Eurocurrency market in the 1960s now enables both firms and governments to borrow (or lend) internationally, on a large scale, in a variety of national monies without regulatory restraint (Witteveen 1982). Except for the late 1960s and early 1970s, the New York capital market has been open to foreign borrowers and depositors.

1

By 1980, exchange controls and other restrictions on capital flows had also been virtually eliminated in the national capital markets of Germany, Britain, and Japan. Thus today's capital market integration parallels that prevailing in world trade in goods and services, whereas in the late 1940s national financial systems were segmented by exchange controls, and Eurocurrency transacting did not yet exist.

Throughout this great transformation, the US dollar has played a peculiarly important role—albeit a changing one. For interbank clearing of 90 percent to 99 percent of international payments, the dollar is the vehicle currency (Kenen 1983). If a Swedish bank wants to buy sterling with marks, it must first buy dollars with marks, and then sterling with dollars.

Aside from gold, which is not readily liquid, most working official reserves of foreign exchange are interest-bearing dollar assets. Since the Marshall Plan in the late 1940s allowed European countries to rebuild their depleted exchange reserves, governments in industrial countries hold mainly US Treasury bonds and bills—and continue to intervene, sometimes heavily, in the interbank market for their currency against dollars. Reflecting these continual interventions under fixed or floating exchange rates, table 1.1 shows the substantial fluctuations in the dollar exchange reserves of the industrial countries over the past twenty years. The substantial exception to this convention is the tendency of some European countries to hold one another's currencies or European Currency Units in the context of a regional exchange rate agreement: the European Monetary System (Bergsten and Williamson 1982).

International trade in primary commodities—such as oil or wheat—is typically invoiced in dollars. On the other hand, each industrial country tends to use its own currency to invoice exports of manufactures and finance trade, although exports to the United States are mainly invoiced in dollars.

In this asymmetrical system, the currencies of less developed countries (LDCs) are not used at all to invoice their foreign trade or capital market transactions. Central banks or treasuries in LDCs hold more of their liquid exchange reserves in Eurodollar deposits than do industrial countries, and now diversify somewhat into other "reserve" currencies—such as deutsche marks and yen. However, LDC governments are big dollar debtors at longer term—especially if government guarantees of private foreign indebtedness are consolidated with official debt. When private Japanese banks lend to Mexico, the loans are typically (although no longer exclusively) denominated in dollars.

TABLE 1.1   Direct dollar liabilities of the United States to foreign central
banks and governments (billion dollars, year-end stocks)

Year	Canada[a]	Japan[b]	Western Europe[c]	Total	Annual percentage change
1963	1.79	1.59	8.51	11.89	
1964	1.81	1.50	9.32	12.63	+6.2
1965	1.70	1.57	8.83	12.10	−4.4
1966	1.33	1.47	7.77	10.57	−14.5
1967	1.31	1.45	10.32	13.08	+23.7
1968	1.87	2.26	8.06	12.19	−7.3
1969	1.62	2.61	7.07	11.30	−7.9
1970	2.95	3.19	13.61	19.75	+74.8
1971	3.98	13.78	30.13	47.89	+142.0
1972	4.25	16.48	34.20	54.93	+14.7
1973	3.85	10.20	45.76	59.81	+8.9
1974	3.66	11.35	44.33	59.34	−0.8
1975	3.13	10.63	45.70	59.46	+0.2
1976	3.41	13.88	45.88	63.17	+6.2
1977	2.33	20.13	70.75	93.21	+47.6
1978	2.49	28.90	93.09	124.48	+33.5
1979	1.90	16.36	85.60	103.86	−19.9
1980	1.56	21.56	81.59	104.71	+0.8
1981	2.40	24.72	65.22	92.34	−11.8
1982	2.08	19.17	60.72	81.97	−11.2
1983, Q3	2.76	20.45	63.25	86.46	+5.5

Source: IMF, *International Financial Statistics, 1982 Yearbook* and February 1983; US
Department of Commerce, *Survey of Current Business*, December 1983.
a. Line 5 aad IFS (United States). Data for 1982 and through third quarter 1983 are derived
from line 57, in "US International Transactions, by Area," *Survey of Current Business*.
b. Because direct US liabilities to the Japanese government were not available, the virtually
identical series on total Japanese reserves in foreign currency was used—line ldd IFS (Japan).
c. Line 5 abd IFS (United States). Data for 1982 and through third quarter 1983 are derived
from line 57, in "US International Transactions, by Area," *Survey of Current Business*.

In his 1983 empirical study, "The Role of the Dollar as an International Currency," Peter B. Kenen summarizes the situation:

There was some decline in the use of the dollar in international trade shortly after the shift to more flexible exchange rates a decade ago, and I ascribe the decline to that shift, not to the weakness of the dollar in the foreign-exchange markets. There has been some significant decline in the use of the dollar as a reserve asset and thus some movement toward a multiple reserve-currency system. But the dollar is still the dominant currency in the international finance system, even in the reserve system narrowly defined. Paraphrasing Mark Twain's remark on hearing that a newspaper had published his obituary, reports of the death of the dollar are greatly exaggerated. (Kenen 1983, p.3)

Finally, the financial position of the United States remains asymmetrical with respect to other countries. Throughout both fixed and floating exchange rates, interventions by the American government in the foreign exchange markets were comparatively infrequent; its reserves of foreign currencies were, and are, negligible. And there is a certain benign logic to a system whereby the center country does *not* have targets for relative currency values that could conflict with the desired dollar exchange rates of a multitude of other governments (Mundell 1969).

Consequently, for descriptive convenience, I shall refer to the postwar monetary system as a "world dollar standard"—with apologies to readers who, somewhat justifiably, do not like its imperial connotations. When the high degree of American autonomy under the present world dollar standard is contrasted with the more cooperative and symmetrical "international standard" proposed in chapter 5, perhaps both labels will seem more apt.

Since the industrial economies abandoned their fixed dollar parities in the early 1970s, the world dollar standard has become less stable. Exchange rates have shown great volatility day-to-day or week-to-week, and a tendency toward misalignment for months or even years (Williamson 1983b). The profitability of investment and production decisions across countries, and within any one country, is now more difficult to calculate. Steady gains in productivity in tradable goods—characteristic of the 1950s and 1960s—have eroded.

Monetary instability has diminished popular support for the ideal of free trade. In 1982–83, for example, the overvalued dollar markedly increased protectionist sentiment in the United States. In particular, quantitative restrictions (more than tariffs) are seen as protective devices to insulate domestic industries from the effects of currency misalignments. Quotas limiting the importation of Japanese automobiles, or of European steel products, tend to make American (dollar) prices in these industries invariant to subsequent exchange rate movements.

Using an exchange rate index plotted quarterly and trade-weighted against 17 trading partners, figure 1.1 shows major fluctuations of the US dollar since 1970: large depreciations in 1971–73 and 1977–78, and the great appreciation of 1981–83. Figure 1.2 shows the sharp fluctuations since 1975 in the exchange rates of Germany, the Netherlands, Japan, and the United Kingdom. The dollar exchange rates of the three European countries fluctuate much more than their "effective" (trade-weighted) exchange rate, which is dominated by official intervention to limit intra-European fluctuations. Japan, not being part of a regional payments agreement, displays large fluctuations in *both* its dollar and effective exchange rates. Neither figure 1.1 nor 1.2 shows the great short-run volatility that accompanied these large quarterly and annual swings in the "floating" dollar.

The world economy suffered major price inflations in 1973–74 and 1979–80, and a major deflation in 1982–83. Each of these episodes followed one of the sharp depreciations or appreciations of the US dollar shown in figure 1.1. That these fluctuations in the American and world price levels were mainly monetary in origin, and not primarily due to exogenous changes in the price of oil, is established empirically in chapter 4.

To understand better why monetary instability is inherent under floating exchange rates, consider first the nature of monetary coordination under the old regime.

The Fixed Rate Dollar Standard

In the 1950s and 1960s, the American government maintained an official gold parity of $35 per ounce through infrequent transactions with other central banks—mainly outside the open exchange market. However, the operational heart of the system of fixed exchange rates was the convention of having other central banks intervene in the open market for foreign exchange in order to keep their currencies within three-quarters of a percent of their dollar parities. To avoid intervention at cross purposes, the Federal Reserve System typically did not intervene in the foreign exchanges. Legal cover for this

FIGURE 1.1   **Movements in the dollar exchange rate (plotted from quarterly averages, 1975-100)**

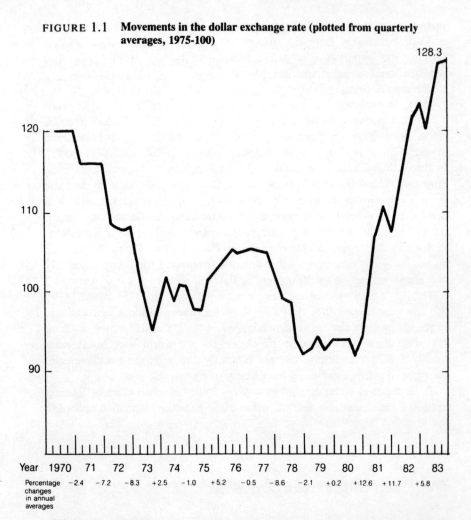

Source: IMF, *International Financial Statistics,* various issues: line amx for the United States. Average trade-weighted value of the dollar measured against 17 currencies of the major industrial trading partners.

fixed rate dollar standard was provided by the Articles of Agreement of the International Monetary Fund.

Occasionally, the IMF sanctioned a discrete change in an official dollar

FIGURE 1.2   Movements in exchange rates

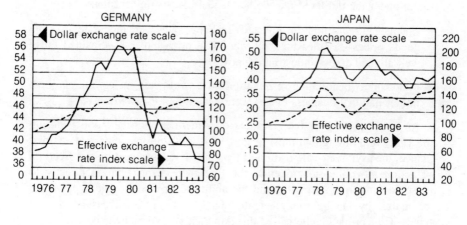

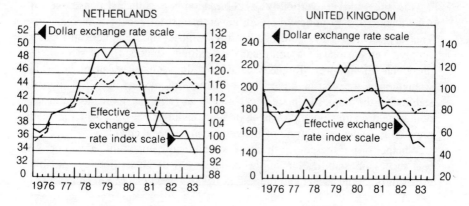

Source: Federal Reserve Bank of St. Louis, "International Economic Conditions," January 1984.

parity: for Britain in 1967, France in 1958 and 1959, and Germany in 1961. More often than not, however, industrial countries adjusted their internal financial policies to preserve the preexisting exchange rate. From 1950 to 1970, the Bank of Japan maintained its exchange rate at 360 yen to the dollar: monetary policy was eased when Japan's balance of payments tended toward surplus and tightened when deficits threatened.[1] Although the industrial

1. Countries that ran balance-of-payments surpluses vis-à-vis the United States were somewhat

countries were not then so highly integrated financially, monetary harmonization under the old fixed rate dollar standard was sufficient that:

• Changes in *real* (inflation adjusted) exchange rates were moderate: tradable goods prices—as measured by wholesale price indices—remained fairly well aligned across industrial countries.

• Major bouts of inflation or deflation on a worldwide scale were avoided: milder national business cycles were generally *not synchronized*.

An understanding of the restraints on American monetary policy during the 1950s and throughout most of the 1960s is, therefore, important. At first glance, the asymmetrical position of the United States gave it unique freedom of action: no obligation to enter the foreign exchange market directly to preserve some official parity, and the ability to finance American payments "deficits" by having foreign central banks acquire US Treasury bills or bonds. General de Gaulle called this America's "exorbitant privilege."

Was the gold convertibility by obligation a significant constraint on American monetary policy? Foreign governments' infrequent conversions of Treasury securities into gold had no direct impact on the American money supply. Yet, visions of a continually dwindling American gold stock kept presidents Eisenhower, Kennedy, and even Johnson awake at night. This strengthened the conservative bias in American monetary policy toward stabilizing the domestic price level—and away from a more adventurous policy of targeting unemployment or real output in the mode of the then prevailing academic doctrine of macroeconomic management.

Whether or not the gold restraint was empirically important,[2] this more or less successful stabilization of the dollar prices of internationally tradable goods through the 1950s into the middle 1960s—see table 4.4 in chapter 4—

less likely to adjust their internal monetary policies than those in deficit, (Michaely 1971). The outstanding example was Germany, which allowed its dollar exchange reserves to accumulate continually in the 1950s and 1960s (at a fairly constant exchange rate) instead of increasing its domestic money supply in an offsetting fashion.

2. Because of the "Triffin Dilemma," the dollar gold exchange standard cannot be reconstructed. Robert Triffin (1960) demonstrated that this system depended on having most of the world's gold concentrated in one country, the United States after World War II. It also depended on having only modest outstanding dollar claims against the center country. As the world economy grew vis-à-vis the center country's gold stock, Triffin showed that the dollar-gold convertibility commitment must break down sooner or later.

was essential in making the fixed rate dollar standard mutually satisfactory. Foreign governments could subordinate their monetary policies to maintaining a fixed dollar parity knowing that the US government would reciprocate by using its degree of freedom to stabilize the dollar's domestic and international purchasing power.

But this limited exercise of American monetary "autonomy" in the 1950s and 1960s had one further essential ingredient. The demand for domestic money in the United States was stable[3]—in comparison to the instability of the 1970s and 1980s. (This important difference between the periods of fixed and floating exchange rates is demonstrated empirically in chapter 4). Therefore, by controlling the American money supply by itself, with no systematic attention paid to the foreign exchange markets, the Federal Reserve System could *unilaterally* stabilize the American price level. Explicit coordination of American monetary policy with that of other central banks was not then necessary to achieve price stability within the United States.

Putting the matter into the familiar framework of domestic monetarism, a fairly close correlation existed in the 1950s and 1960s between changes in US nominal GNP and changes in the US money supply lagged a year or two. With somewhat longer lags, there was a predictable effect of US money on American prices. Consequently, control over the American money supply—without reference to the foreign exchanges—seemed to monetarists to be sufficient to stabilize the American economy. What monetarists didn't (and still don't) realize is that the underlying stability of the demand for money in the United States in the 1950s and 1960s was itself peculiar to the fixed exchange rate regime, and to the absence of competing international reserve currencies.

Floating Exchange Rates and the Breakdown of Monetary Coordination

After the transition to floating exchange rates in the 1970s and 1980s, how was this mutual monetary adjustment among the industrial countries altered?

In the 1960s, academic economists had generally favored increased exchange flexibility in order to promote national monetary independence! Sovereignty in monetary matters was then thought to be an advantage in

---

3. What a "stable" demand for domestic money means is analyzed explicitly in chapter 3.

managing the economy toward full employment without inflation. Formal exchange rate obligations, to which national monetary policy had been subordinated, were (correctly) seen as an obstacle to autonomous control over the *supply* of the national money. By letting the exchange rates float to balance international payments, each country could ostensibly direct monetary (and fiscal) policy toward whatever degree of domestic inflation or unemployment seemed appropriate.

Whether this insular viewpoint was ever valid for economies smaller and more open than the US economy in the 1950s and 1960s is doubtful. After 1970, however, the absence of officially fixed exchange parities, and of any firm commitment to international monetary coordination, led to waves of international currency speculation. According to their changing assessments of future inflation and political stability, international investors—multinational firms, Arab sheiks, central banks in LDCs, and so on—continually shifted their portfolio preferences among sterling, mark, yen, Swiss franc, and dollar assets. Such portfolio shifts and associated exchange rate changes destabilized the *demand* for each national money (chapter 3), and led to self-fulfilling prophecies of inflation or deflation.

More than most academic economists, central bankers in open economies understand the importance of gearing domestic monetary policy toward exchange rate stabilization. Even after the suspension of official dollar parities, industrial countries except the United States have sometimes allowed their money growth to be fast or slow depending on the strength or weakness of their currencies in foreign exchanges. On several occasions in the 1970s and 1980s, they altered their domestic money growth to offset partially sharp changes in their dollar exchange rates (chapter 4).

After 1970, only the Federal Reserve System—at the center of the world dollar standard—conducted monetary policy without reference to the foreign exchanges. (As discussed in chapter 5, the one significant exception could be the rapid growth in US M1 from the summer of 1982 to the summer of 1983, when the dollar was obviously greatly overvalued.) Indeed, table 4.1 in chapter 4 shows that the Fed normally chose to exercise its supply-side autonomy under floating rates by having smoother annual money growth than any other industrial country as if it had chosen to follow the principle of "domestic monetarism!" Consequently, the American cycle of boom and bust of the past dozen years is primarily due to instability in the demand for dollar assets (as shown empirically in chapter 4) and the failure of the Fed to accommodate these demands by adjusting US money growth toward stabilizing the dollar exchange rate.

Why should the American business cycle have had worldwide effects? The reason is the peculiar asymmetry between the Fed's behavior and that of the European and Japanese central banks. When the dollar was weak, other central banks tended to expand their money supplies while the Fed failed to contract. The result was a net increase in "world" money preceding each of the two great inflations in the 1970s. Conversely, when the dollar became unexpectedly strong as in 1980–82, the others tended to contract without any offsetting monetary expansion in the United States. Together with the adverse wealth effect from an overvalued dollar on dollar debtors in the Third World, the decline in world money growth in 1980–81 contributed to the worldwide deflation of 1982–83.

This inverse relationship between the strength of the dollar in the exchange markets and changes in *foreign* money growth after 1970 (chapter 4) contributed to the unfortunate *synchronization* of the American business cycle with that of other countries. Feedback effects from this imbalance then magnified inflations and deflations within the United States itself. However, the problem can be remedied by agreeing on a more symmetrical monetary relationship between the United States and the other major industrial economies—as discussed in chapter 5. First, however, let us analyze more deeply where conventional macroeconomic doctrines went astray.

2 The Insular Tradition in Macroeconomic Theory

Western industrial economies have become more open to foreign trade in assets as well as in goods, but accepted theories of macroeconomic policy, whether Keynesian or monetarist, have lagged behind this internationalization process. Widespread adherence to the concept of national autonomy in monetary matters—particularly in the United States—is more in keeping with an *insular economy:* one with limited financial and commodity arbitrage with the outside world but not one fully closed to foreign trade.

This insular tradition implicitly underlies the arguments still used in favor of floating exchange rates, on one hand, and suggestions for reinsulating national financial systems by imposing some form of exchange controls, on the other. It led to ill-chosen monetary policies in the United States, Britain, and elsewhere during the 1970s. An analysis of this dominance of the insular tradition in accepted macroeconomic theory, even as the ambit of international trade increased, logically precedes discussion of how monetary harmonization might come about.

The Importance of Capital Mobility for Free Trade

In general, any hard currency country maintaining an open monetary system, in which foreigners can invoice their foreign trade and freely transact on capital account, provides an international "public good." Private export credits at commercial rates of interest, and low-cost hedging facilities for covering foreign exchange risk, are greatly facilitated. The world needs at least one major country[1] willing to provide this service if international trade

---

1. Or some international agency capable of creating a stable-valued money that is generally accepted for financing private commodity trade and capital transfers. However, the creation of an independent and purely international money is technically very difficult to accomplish (McKinnon 1979, pp. 270–91).

13

is to be monetized and multilateral, rather than bartered on a truncated bilateral basis. And, apart from the old British sterling area, under the early postwar dollar standard, that one country was the United States.

However, having only one financially open country does not ensure an efficient distribution of saving and investment throughout the world economy. The efficient transfer of surplus saving from natural creditor countries to natural debtors requires that other market-oriented economies also remove their restrictions on capital account transactions. Assuming that international monetary equilibrium is maintained (a big proviso, dealt with in chapters 3 and 4), trade surpluses then reflect surplus saving. Private capital automatically flows inward to finance trade deficits and outward to finance trade surpluses. *With smoothly functioning capital markets, little or no change in the "real" exchange rate is necessary to transfer saving from one country to another.*

For example, when oil was discovered in Alaska in the 1960s and became profitable to develop in the early 1970s, there was a big capital inflow to finance drilling and the Alaska pipeline. Because the Alaskan dollar was fixed to the American dollar with free currency convertibility, the Alaskan money supply immediately expanded and expenditures increased such as to create a big trade deficit (before the oil came on stream). True, the "real" exchange rate slowly appreciated over some years as oil companies bid up wages and the prices of other "nontradable" services in Alaska. But no appreciation in the nominal exchange rate between the Alaskan dollar and the US dollar was needed to effect the transfer smoothly.[2]

Consequently, having two countries with currency convertibility on capital account is better than one, and three is better than two, and so on. With many countries' monetary systems so liberalized, however, the potential problem is that other fully convertible currencies would challenge the US dollar's dominant position as a reserve currency. Portfolio switching from one country to another in response to political or economic news can, under floating exchange rates, cause severe exchange rate misalignment. Unfortunately, capital account restrictions, whether or not they are designed to correct such misalignments, interfere with the natural process of finance for the net trade balance.

To correct the overvalued dollar in the early 1980s, the European and

---

2. Nor would it have been desirable, judging by what happened to Britain when sterling was allowed to appreciate precipitately during the British oil boom of 1979–80—as described in chapter 3.

Japanese governments have come under pressure to restrain their capital outflows by taxes or exchange controls as a "second-best" solution to the currency misalignment (Bergsten 1983). But once imposed, such restrictions would interfere with channeling European, and particularly Japanese, surplus saving to the Third World. Instead, a coordinated monetary system that makes controls on capital movements unnecessary is the preferred solution.

This basic complementarity between free commodity trade and unfettered capital flows eliminates one suggested remedy for macroeconomic instability: the reinsulation of national financial systems from international influences. In the insular Keynesian tradition, James Tobin has proposed "to throw sand in the all too perfect currency-exchange mechanisms, in the hope of filtering out speculative noise and allowing more macroeconomic independence" (Tobin 1982, p. 116). Franco Modigliani (1973) and Rudiger Dornbusch (1983) have had similar thoughts, as have Kareken and Wallace (1981) with their notion of "portfolio autarky." That sand in the world's money machine would be interest rate "equalization" taxes or exchange controls on movements of portfolio capital—very much what John Maynard Keynes himself had in mind when they were legitimized in the 1944 Bretton Woods Agreement, which he helped to negotiate.

While still influential, this Keynes-Tobin view of the desirability of exchange controls is not now typical. Most economists oppose restrictions on capital flows that disrupt international payments on capital or current account.

The Advocacy of Floating Exchange Rates

How then can liberalism in international finance and trade best be reconciled with the desire for national macroeconomic autonomy over domestic prices, income, and employment?

A floating exchange rate is one in which the domestic monetary authority neither intervenes in the foreign exchange markets nor adjusts the domestic money supply toward smoothing exchange rate fluctuations. The majority of economists—whether Keynesians or monetarists—have favored floating, i.e., freely flexible exchange rates. Floating seemed the most efficient way of balancing international payments, while freeing domestic monetary and fiscal policies to pursue domestic macroeconomic objectives. In the postwar period, this view seemed plausible a priori to economists who had no experience with generalized floating.

There were exceptions to this academic consensus favoring floating exchange rates. The concept of an optimum currency area (Mundell 1961; McKinnon 1963) had been applied to (very) small and highly open countries: Panama is better off to maintain a fixed exchange rate with the US dollar and to give up the idea of national monetary autonomy. Within the European Community, few would dispute the efficacy of Belgium's fixed exchange rate with the deutsche mark in the 1970s, and the subordination of Belgian macroeconomic policy to maintaining it.[3]

For major industrial economies, however, Keynesians such as James Meade (1955) and monetarists such as Milton Friedman (1953) and Harry Johnson (1972) argued for floating exchange rates as if the economy under consideration could be insulated from international macroeconomic disturbances. I quote from "The Case for Flexible Exchange Rates, 1969" by Harry G. Johnson, because it is unusually pungent and more contemporary than the earlier articles of Friedman or Meade, while being in broad agreement with both. First comes the primacy of national macroeconomic autonomy.

The fundamental argument for flexible exchange rates is that they would allow countries autonomy with respect to their use of monetary, fiscal and other policy instruments, consistent with the maintenance of whatever degree of freedom in international transactions they choose to allow their citizens, by automatically ensuring the preservation of external equilibrium. (Johnson 1972, p. 199)

Next comes Johnson's presumption that nations remain insulated from each other by standards of domestic trade and commerce: the basis for his argument against fixed exchange rates.

The argument for fixed exchange rates is that they will similarly encourage the integration of the national markets that compose the world economy into an international network of connected markets with similarly beneficial effects on economic efficiency and growth . . . .

In the international economy the movement of labour is certainly subject to serious barriers created by national immigration policies (and in some cases restraints on emigration as well), and the freedom of movement of capital is also restricted by

---

3. Indeed, Belgium's previously successful macroeconomic policies seem to be unraveling in the 1980s. Price inflation is now higher in Belgium than in Germany, with consequential devaluations of the Belgian franc against the deutsche mark.

tariffs and other barriers to trade . . . . The existence of these barriers means that the system of fixed exchange rates does not really establish the equivalent of a single international money, in the sense of a currency whose purchasing power and usefulness tends to equality throughout the market area. (Johnson 1972, p. 202)

To be sure, the advocates of floating recognized that general inflation in one country will eventually make devaluation of that country's currency inevitable but this merely highlights another potential argument for flexible exchange rates. Johnson emphasizes the advantages for macroeconomic autonomy of differing rates of price inflation that allow countries to select different trade-offs between inflation and employment.

On the one hand, a great rift exists between nations like the United Kingdom and the United States, which are anxious to maintain high levels of employment and are prepared to pay a price for it in terms of domestic inflation, and other nations, notably the West German Federal Republic, which are strongly averse to inflation. Under the present fixed exchange-rate system, these nations are pitched against each other in a battle over the rate of inflation that is to prevail in the world economy, since the fixed rate system diffuses the rate of inflation to all the countries involved in it. Flexible rates would allow each country to pursue the mixture of unemployment and price trend objectives it prefers, consistent with international equilibrium, equilibrium being secured by appreciation of the currencies of "price-stability" countries relative to currencies of "full-employment" countries. (Johnson 1972, p. 210)

How innocent we were regarding the trade-off between price inflation and employment! Even if economies could remain insulated, we now understand that having individual countries pursue rates of price inflation different from zero—and, perforce, different from each other—is unnecessarily destabilizing. This old macroeconomic argument in favor of exchange flexibility is no longer credible.

As a corollary to this insular view based on the absence of internationally integrated capital markets, Friedman (who held no illusions about the trade-off between output and employment), Johnson and Meade—as well as Machlup (1972) and Haberler (1949)—all saw the exchange rate as the primary instrument for balancing international trade in goods and services.[4]

---

4. For a more complete critical review of the (insular) empirical assumptions underlying the "elasticities approach" to the balance of trade, see McKinnon 1981.

The exchange rate would be determined through adjustments in trade *flows*: depreciations would quickly boost exports and reduce imports (and vice versa) so that any depreciation would be self-limiting.[5] Substantial movement in exchange rates—although not nearly as much as actually experienced in the 1970s and 1980s—was considered in the 1960s to be both normal and helpful.

Among insular economies, there is a case for continuously balancing imports and exports through ongoing adjustments in the nominal (and real) exchange rate. Indeed, the net trade balance should be kept close to zero if there are no flows of private capital to finance trade deficits or surpluses, or to effect the automatic harmonization of national monetary policies if the exchange rate were fixed. This apparent need for exchange rate flexibility seemed plausible in the late 1940s and early 1950s when private international flows of financial capital were virtually moribund.

In contrast, among the financially open economies of the 1980s, trade deficits and surpluses are better balanced by offsetting automatically flows of private capital—much like the balance achieved between Texas and California. Changes in the exchange rate are neither necessary nor desirable—particularly sharp jumps due to shifts in international asset preferences. But this tranquility in the foreign exchanges when capital markets are open depends critically on proper monetary coordination with neighboring countries—as we shall see.

---

5. They did not understand the principle of the "J-curve" (MaGee 1973): initially, the trade balance moves perversely and only adjusts to exchange rate changes with long lags. The resulting exchange rate instability is only partially offset by the automatic short-run capital flows (McKinnon 1983a).

3 The Exchange Rate as a Monetary Indicator

In this chapter, let us defer for a while the larger problem of coordinating monetary policies over more than one country. That is taken up in chapters 4 and 5. Consider the narrower problem of optimum monetary management in an industrial economy, with an open financial and foreign trade system, while ignoring the impact of its actions on the rest of the world (ROW). In so narrowing the analytical focus, I shall initially assume that ROW's price level is relatively stable as if some organized international monetary standard were operative. Can we then show that orienting domestic monetary policy toward stabilizing the *nominal* exchange rate is in the best interests of the country in question?

In order to motivate the theory to follow, consider some empirical evidence. In *Flexible Exchange Rates in Historical Perspective* (1982), Peter Bernholz covers three centuries of European and American experiences with floating fiat monies. After analyzing more than a dozen historical episodes for highly diverse countries, Bernholz identifies an amazingly consistent empirical regularity: major exchange rate depreciations precede major domestic price inflations. Conversely, sharp appreciations (or slowdowns in the rate of depreciation) signal future deflation and perhaps depression. That movement in a floating exchange rate is an excellent *leading indicator* of future price inflation or deflation also holds true for the United States of the 1970s and 1980s—as is shown in chapter 4.

Secondly, the great variance in exchange rates of the past dozen years has been largely unanticipated by the market (Frenkel and Mussa 1980). Forward exchange rates or (uncovered) interest differentials have been very poor predictors of future spot rates. Apparently, any *news*—whether it be political, monetary, or related to trade flows (such as a new mineral discovery)—which could move the floating exchange rate in the future is immediately telescoped back into the present by international investors quickly switching their preferences between domestic and foreign currency assets. A characteristic of a no-parity regime, therefore, is that the spot exchange rate is very sensitive to hitherto unforeseen changes in the position of the domestic economy vis-à-vis the outside world.

Together, these empirical observations suggest that the central bank could use the exchange rate as a source of information—a monetary indicator—of whether current policy was too tight or too easy. Still necessary, however, is a comprehensive theory of why seemingly nonmonetary forces—political, fiscal, or "real" variations in imports or exports—acting on the exchange rate also call for an official monetary response.

The Proper Objective of Monetary Policy

Fiat money has no intrinsic value other than what the issuing government (central bank) manages to establish. Though differing with Milton Friedman over monetary strategy—whether exchange rates should float and whether the rate of growth in domestic money should be fixed—let us adopt his same basic objective. *The long-run goal of monetary policy is to stabilize the purchasing power of the national money, while avoiding short-run cycles of inflation or deflation.* And, in an open economy, stabilizing money's purchasing power over internationally tradable goods and services is important for securing the domestic price level in the longer run and for preventing undue short-run variance in relative prices between domestic and foreign goods from extraneous monetary disturbances.

Assigning responsibility to the central bank for stabilizing the national money's purchasing power may seem excessively narrow to many readers concerned with unemployment, national output growth, or fluctuations in interest rates. Yet, a strong case can be made (Friedman 1968) that a monetary policy oriented toward price-level stabilization will, incidentally, be quite successful at output and employment stabilization. For an open economy, eliminating sharp fluctuations in the "real" exchange rate due to monetary imbalances would also tend to reduce frictional unemployment and prevent investment misallocation between sheltered and internationally exposed industries. So too would sustained price-level and exchange rate stability tend to eliminate ever-changing premia for inflationary expectations in the term structure of interest rates.

Most important, the stipulation that the government prevent surprise inflations or deflations in the general price level is very strong in a countercyclical sense. The central bank must take resolute expansionary action when an unexpected deflation threatens, and vice versa. Similarly, if the central bank mistakenly allowed a major exchange rate misalignment to occur, it has the responsibility to correct it. These two aspects of price stabilization turn out to be mutually complementary.

On the other hand, asking the monetary authority to target nonmonetary or "real" variables is not feasible. Unemployment depends on wage-setting conditions in the labor market that the central bank can't control. Real (inflation-adjusted) interest rates, the current account surplus in foreign trade, and growth in real income, depend on the balance between saving and investment in the national and world economies; in recent years, this balance has depended heavily on current and projected fiscal deficits. Assigning the central bank to target these nonmonetary objectives is destined to fail, while incurring substantial risk of cyclical instability or even a breakdown in the financial system.

Imposing our objective of price stability is only reasonable if the central bank can, itself, control the monetary system. In many countries around the world, either large public sector deficits, or large-scale forced lending by the banking system to favored borrowers (usually at less-than-market rates of interest), effectively undermines this control. Price-level and exchange rate stability is not then a feasible objective—as the recent inflationary experiences of Italy and Portugal, among many other countries, would suggest.

Consequently, our analysis will be confined to potential hard currency countries: open economies whose domestic financial processes are sufficiently robust that each central bank can independently control the supply of domestic money. Either primary securities markets are sufficiently developed—as in Canada, Germany, Japan, the Netherlands, Switzerland, the United States, and the United Kingdom—that the government can sell nonmonetary debt to the nonbank public to finance government expenditures, or fiscal deficits themselves are small and inconsequential. These hard currency economies are, after all, dominant in international trade and finance—and set the tone for monetary developments elsewhere.

Keying Monetary Policy on the Nominal Exchange Rate

Knowing that the exchange rate is highly sensitive to political-economic news and to current domestic monetary conditions, the central bank can harness this information to increase the efficiency of domestic monetary policy. How can such information be efficiently processed?

At any point, the authorities observe movements in the nominal exchange rate; or, if the government is actively defending the rate, they observe incipient pressure in the foreign exchanges. However, the authorities themselves are never sure of the underlying reasons for the shift in portfolio preferences by international investors. Without assuming any such official omniscience, suppose the central bank follows the simple rule: *increase the money supply above its long-run norm when the exchange rate appreciates and reduce the domestic money supply when depreciation threatens.*[1] It turns out that this rule is remarkably robust in improving the efficiency of domestic monetary policy.

However, for the *current* nominal exchange rate to be unambiguously successful as the monetary indicator, two further assumptions are required:

(i) in the hard currency outside world on which the central bank is keying, the general price level for internationally tradable goods remains stable

(ii) the domestic economy is (begins in) full financial equilibrium with no inflation or deflation in process. At the prevailing exchange rate, the domestic price level is properly aligned with the outside world.

Somewhat surprisingly, most of the advantages of gearing national monetary policy toward the exchange rate still hold even if assumptions (i) and (ii) are violated. But then, in order to avoid over- or undervaluation of the "real" exchange rate, the central bank must continually recalculate its appropriate target for the nominal exchange rate. This important issue is taken up in chapter 5. For now, let us presume that both assumptions hold, and go on to analyze various disturbances in the foreign exchange market as if the current nominal exchange rate were the appropriate monetary indicator.

One further analytical simplification is warranted. Suppose we don't specify what money supply technique the central bank uses in responding to the exchange rate indicator. Our analysis is invariant as to *how* the domestic money supply is changed. When the domestic currency came under downward pressure in the foreign exchanges, the central bank could:

---

1. Which could be judged by some trend rate of growth, such as a Friedman rule.

- raise the discount rate in the traditional manner and reduce lending to the commercial banks

- sell domestic treasury bonds or bills in the open market to reduce base money in circulation

- repurchase domestic base money with foreign exchange, i.e., nonsterilized intervention

- use any combination of the above.

Essentially, I am assuming that relatively small changes in the outstanding stock of domestic base money have sufficient leverage on the domestic banking system—through reserve requirements and the general importance of liquid cash—that the financial consequences of changing the money supply far outweigh any secondary effects in the stocks of other financial assets—the huge portfolios of domestic or foreign bonds outstanding. Only changes in the liabilities side of the central bank's balance sheet are deemed to be empirically important in stabilizing the exchange rate.[2]

Conversely, suppose the economy starts from a position where the exchange rate is stable. What then are the consequences of any such changes in the supply of central bank money? As in the standard model of liquidity preference, domestic interest rates fall if the money supply is unexpectedly increased. With a given money demand schedule, where the interest rate on domestic bonds is the opportunity cost to domestic holders of money, a sudden increase in the money supply must reduce the rate of interest—as shown in the upper panel of figure 3.1.

But any tendency for the domestic interest rate to fall will upset the portfolios of international investors. They will switch from domestic to foreign bonds and induce the domestic currency to depreciate. Moreover, the immediate exchange depreciation may be quite violent in the sense of *overshooting* its long-run equilibrium level (Dornbusch 1976). Hence either the exchange depreciation, or the lower domestic interest rate, tells the central bank that money has become "easy." Because the economy began in full financial equilibrium, both would indicate that the central bank had made a mistake and should now contract.

---

2. Direct nonsterilized intervention in the foreign exchanges may be preferred when the country has a very precisely defined official parity in the middle of a narrow band. The distinction between less precise and more precise exchange rate targets is taken up in chapter 5.

FIGURE 3.1   **The domestic money market, the exchange rate, and the price level**

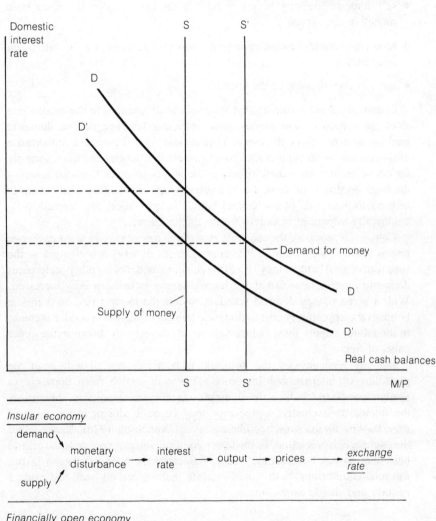

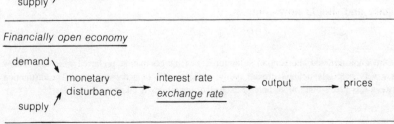

In the Keynesian tradition, this analysis can be turned on its head. Suppose there is some instability in domestic liquidity preference: the (ex ante) velocity of domestic money changes at the prevailing interest rate. The demand by commercial banks for excess reserves held with the central bank could change; so too could private citizens decide to alter their ratio of checking accounts to coin and currency.

If liquidity preference suddenly falls—the leftward shift in the demand-for-money function portrayed in the upper panel of figure 3.1—the domestic interest rate again decreases. This upsets the portfolio balance of international investors and causes exchange rate depreciation. Again the central bank gets the same (correct) signal from both the domestic interest rate and the exchange rate: money is too easy. If an offsetting monetary contraction isn't under-taken—with the incidental effect of restoring the initial exchange rate—the economy will suffer a bout of domestic price inflation after a lag of some months or years.

Clearly, with disturbances confined to the domestic money supply or to the domestic demand-for-money schedule, *with no autonomous shifts in expectations about the future,* the domestic interest rate and exchange rate are equally good leading indicators of inflationary potential. (The exchange rate only becomes the preferred indicator in the face of exogenous changes in inflationary expectations—or in other speculations on the future—as we shall see.)

That a floating exchange rate is immediately sensitive to any change in domestic monetary conditions is now well accepted in the recent technical literature on the subject. In the 1950s and 1960s, however, this was not commonly perceived by the persuasive advocates of floating. Because of their implicit assumption of an insular economy, they believed that any domestic monetary expansion would increase output and then prices, *followed by* (or coincident with) a compensating depreciation in the foreign exchanges. (See the quotations from Harry Johnson in chapter 2.) Therefore, they did not see that the exchange rate could be a useful barometer of the stance of current monetary policy—much less that it would incorporate news about the future.

The lower panel of figure 3.1 shows the effect of some sudden monetary disturbance (taken from the upper panel) on the domestic exchange rate, output and prices—the order of causation and lag structure are indicated by the arrows. Note that in the financially open economy, the exchange rate is affected first and prices last, whereas those arrows shown for the insular economy reverse the order of causation. In any financially open economy, therefore, a floating exchange rate is a good indicator of current ease or tightness in the national money market. Conversely, our monetary rule (as sketched above) is more than sufficient to keep the exchange rate within some narrow range.

"Nonmonetary" Influences on the Exchange Rate

Many readers may object to the idea of stabilizing the nominal exchange rate (against a stable-valued foreign currency) in order to secure monetary control. After all, shouldn't the nominal exchange rate be free to fluctuate to compensate for "real" disturbances in international trade?

Surprisingly, no. As long as domestic monetary policy is convincingly subordinated to maintaining a stable nominal exchange rate, international flows of financial capital will automatically offset deficits or surpluses in the balance of trade. However, if the exchange rate is floating, real shocks in international trade or capital movements are likely to upset the economy's monetary equilibrium!

To see this important point, let us take representative examples of seemingly nonmonetary shocks that have hit the industrial economies over the past several decades. By "nonmonetary," I mean any disturbance other than a shift in the current money supply or money demand schedules.

What exogenous shocks—or news—might upset the portfolio balance of international investors? Consider the following three broad categories that would make domestic bonds seem riskier and induce a capital outflow:

- *Political risk:* fear of exchange controls, wealth taxes, war, or other factors that bear on the convenience of holding assets in the domestic currency as distinct from foreign money

- *Inflation risk* in the longer term: an assessment of increased future domestic price inflation, with exchange depreciation, relative to that prevailing in alternative hard currency countries

- *Real exchange rate risk* due, say, to an unexpected decline in the international terms of trade and in future current account surpluses. For example, a fall in the price of oil reduces the attractiveness of assets denominated in a "petrocurrency" if the exchange rate is floating.

Often, individual investors might not distinguish sharply between political risk and inflation risk in the longer term. Suppose the future election of a radical populist government suddenly appears more likely. Domestic investors don't really know what will hit them harder: new taxes on wealth or future price inflation and exchange depreciation. Whether or not they make this distinction, their willingness to hold domestic financial assets sharply decreases in favor of goods or foreign exchange. Unless the central bank contracts the money supply and allows nominal interest rates to rise and compensate for the increased riskiness of holding domestic financial assets, the real interest rate will decline because the future is being discounted more sharply. With the current money supply unchanged, this fall in the real interest rate and the exchange rate depreciation will aggravate whatever domestic price inflation was going to occur anyway.

Consider now an unexpected real shock to an oil-exporting country which is the inverse of the third point, above. In 1979, Britons suddenly found that the anticipated future stream of foreign exchange earnings was substantially greater because of an unexpected increase in the international price of oil. Because sterling was floating, international investors projected that the future foreign exchange value of sterling would be higher. They immediately telescoped this information back into 1979, and sharply bid up the nominal (and real) British exchange rate, greatly reducing the international competitiveness of British industry. The result was a precipitate fall in the previously anticipated rate of inflation and a depression in 1980–81 that the British authorities had not expected.

Clearly, the correct response in 1979 by the Bank of England to this real disturbance would have been to increase the British money supply beyond its preplanned rate of growth in order to stabilize the nominal (and real) exchange rate. Nominal interest rates on sterling bonds would have fallen— correctly reflecting the lessened exchange and inflation risk perceived by investors. The rise in the real rate of interest on sterling assets, and the unexpectedly sharp decline in economic activity, would then have been avoided.[3]

Ambiguous Monetary Signals from the Interest Rate

In considering these disturbances to expectations about the future course of the open economy, the nominal exchange rate gave the right signal to the monetary authorities, whereas the nominal interest rate was ambiguous.

---

3. Of course, if sudden deflation, rather than a more gradual disinflation, was deemed desirable, then the Bank of England's unresponsiveness to the oil shock is more defensible.

With the inflation scare, the domestic interest rate increases—if only incipiently in the short run—and (incorrectly) signals that money is possibly too tight. In the intermediate term, if inflation were allowed to proceed and reduce real money balances, nominal interest rates would increase even further. Reflecting expected future inflation, this well-known "Fisher" premium in nominal interest rates could well be more pronounced in an open economy where domestic investors have easy access to *foreign* financial assets as a convenient hedge against inflation. In an insular economy where (inconvenient) physical assets were the natural inflation hedge, Fisher premia in interest rates would be less volatile.

Similarly, in the 1979 British example of an increase in the price of oil, some (incipient) initial decline in the sterling rate of interest could have resulted from the suddenly higher investor demand for sterling bonds.[4] Nevertheless, any such fall in the interest rate could not be taken as a signal that money in Britain had become too easy! Quite the contrary. The appreciation of sterling in the foreign exchanges was giving the right signal that a monetary expansion was warranted.

Changes in nominal interest rates accurately reflect what the central bank should do only in the case of shifts in the *current* money demand or money supply functions as they appear in the upper panel of figure 3.1. Then an increase in the interest rate (and exchange rate) correctly indicates that money is too tight and vice versa. But once interest rates move in anticipation of some *future* change in a country's political-economic or monetary regime, they become worse than useless for helping the central bank decide what it should do today.

Because the central bank is not omniscient in understanding what is roiling the financial markets at any point in time, knowing that the exchange rate gives an unambiguous monetary signal is a big advantage—remembering our caveat that the economy is starting from a position of financial equilibrium.

Fiscal Policy

Another kind of nonmonetary shock is an unexpected change in *discretionary* domestic fiscal policy likely to prevail in the future. For example, a sharp

---

4. While clear in principle, this example was somewhat muddied in practice by the Bank of England's tightening of monetary policy in 1979–80 that caused nominal rates of interest actually to increase.

increase in projected future budget deficits occurred in France in early 1981 with the Mitterrand election, and in 1981 into early 1982 in the United States, when Reagan tax cuts were not matched by equivalent expenditure reductions. Is a stable exchange rate, based on a variable money supply, still the right response by the monetary authority when these new expectations first make themselves felt in the foreign exchanges? Again yes, but a complete analysis of how fiscal policy works itself out in an open economy is beyond the scope of this monograph.

Nevertheless, such fiscal shocks fit roughly into the above taxonomy of nonmonetary disturbances. Much depends on whether or not the central bank is expected to finance prospective deficits by new money issue in the near-term future. If yes, the Mitterrand case, then the result is analogous to the longer term inflation scare analyzed above. The franc came under immediate downward pressure in early 1981, correctly indicating that the Bank of France should, at that time, have restricted the money supply and increased interest rates in order to avoid future inflation.

If no monetization of the deficit is expected, the Reagan case, the result is analogous to the inverse real exchange rate risk analyzed above. There is an anticipated sharp increase in the inflow of foreign exchange from abroad: overseas sales of US Treasury bonds increase although near-term US money growth does not. In the Reagan case, the projected unmonetized fiscal deficits increased (real) rates of interest on dollar assets and contributed to (but by no means were the only cause of) the great upward pressure on the US dollar in the foreign exchanges in 1981 and early 1982. Again, the exchange rate clearly signaled that the Federal Reserve should have expanded the US money supply to prevent the dollar from appreciating so sharply; the depression of 1982 in the United States would then have been mitigated.[5]

Paradoxically, under a floating exchange rate, an *anticipated* increase in an unmonetized fiscal deficit tends to depress the domestic macroeconomy in the short run; when and if the deficit is actually realized in the longer run, it might be expansionary although with lags of uncertain duration (Burgstaller 1983; Ambler 1984). The boom in the United States in 1983 and early 1984 could, in part, reflect this delayed fiscal effect—although rapid monetary expansion provides an equally plausible explanation, as shown in chapter 4.

---

5. The empirical relationship of American monetary policy to the dollar exchange rate is analyzed more fully in chapter 4. It should also be noted that a large unmonetized fiscal deficit eventually will cause a large trade deficit whether the exchange rate is fixed or floating. And the American trade deficit became very large in 1983–84.

The advantages of fixing the nominal exchange rate in response to these fiscal, political, or terms of trade disturbances become clearer once one realizes that international portfolio preferences themselves are more volatile when the exchange rate is floating. People continually speculate on changes in future monetary cum exchange rate policy as new economic information becomes available. On the other hand, once the exchange rate is convincingly fixed, continual speculative movement from domestic to foreign currency bonds (or vice versa) is pointless. In effect, the subordination of monetary policy to the exchange rate reduces uncertainty about what future monetary policy will be, because speculators know that the central bank(s) is (are) committed to maintain current relative currency values.

The Principle of Indirect Currency Substitution

Many readers will still be unhappy with the subordination of domestic monetary policy to the needs of a fixed exchange rate. After all, the primary job of any central bank is to balance supply with the (possibly fluctuating) demand for domestic money at a stable price level. But how does the demand for domestic transactions balances—and the derived demand for base money— increase just because the international demand for domestic bonds suddenly increases? Why should changes in international portfolio preferences between *nonmonetary assets* affect the demand for domestic *money?* The short answer is that the demand for domestic transactions balances increases *indirectly* when international investors desire more bonds denominated in the domestic currency.[6]

To understand better the overall consequences of these indirect changes in the demand for money, let us now consider two mutually open economies of similar size. Suppose countries A and B are in domestic and international portfolio balance, domestic prices are stable, and the exchange rate is maintaining purchasing power parity (PPP) between the two national price levels. Let S = currency A/currency B be the actual exchange rate, and let S^{PPP} be its equilibrium rate. Initially, $S = S^{PPP}$.

---

6. The reader should note that my argument here is not generally accepted. The conventional view is that switches in bond preferences warrant sterilized official intervention to stabilize the exchange rate, but no change in the money supply (Dornbusch, 1983; Henderson 1982). This counter argument is discussed in the annex to this chapter.

Let B_a be the bonds of country A yielding the nominal interest rate i_a and B_b denote the bonds of country B yielding i_b.

Now suppose international investors respond to some sudden political or economic news by shifting their desired portfolio from B_a to B_b. If some force—either the government itself or the belief of private foreign exchange dealers that the government is committed to defending exchange equilibrium— temporarily maintains $S = S^{PPP}$, i_a will tend to increase and i_b to decline. But this upward pressure on i_a is then transmitted through the domestic liquidity preference function (the function describing the demand for money by domestic transactors) to the demand for noninterest-bearing domestic money, M_a. This incipient increase in i_a causes an incipient fall in the demand for M_a by domestic transactors. Disturbances in the international bond market are thereby transmitted to the national money market.

However, so long as the central bank in A takes no action to reduce the supply of M_a, A's private sector can't reduce its actual money holdings and i_a can't actually increase. With M_a unchanged, the attempt by domestic transactors to switch from M_a to B_a simply drives i_a back down to where it started—as if the domestic interest rate were in a liquidity trap.[7] Because the initial decline in the demand for M_a cannot be realized, the temporary increase in i_a (reflecting the risk premia being required by international investors to hold bonds in currency A) cannot be sustained and neither can our equilibrium exchange rate. S rises sufficiently far above S^{PPP} until disturbed international investors believe that some significant future decline (appreciation of currency A) is likely. Only after overshooting has progressed far enough, and regressive exchange rate expectations have set in, is the willingness of international investors to hold B_a restored.

For a closed economy, we know that a fall in the demand for money is inflationary if its supply remains unchanged. And in our open economy A, the shift in international portfolio preference from B_a to B_b is also inflationary— unless the national money supply is contracted. The primary mechanism of inflation is the depreciation of A's currency in the foreign exchanges: the direct inflationary impact on the prices of internationally traded commodities *and* the unmistakable signal that price inflation will be greater in the future. On the other hand, an unexpected deflation in country B occurs—as if the

---

7. For a further analysis of this idea of a liquidity trap, see McKinnon (1983b). In effect, interest rates are not free to reflect accurately changing assessments of international riskiness unless the national money supply changes with international portfolio preferences.

demand for money had sharply risen there—unless its central bank increases M_b in an offsetting fashion.

In summary, the shift from B_a to B_b in the international bond market has the effect of *indirect currency substitution:* as if private agents collectively were reducing their demand for M_a and increasing their demand for M_b (McKinnon 1982). People want to be less liquid in country A and more liquid in country B. This process of indirect currency substitution suggests why the international coordination of A's and B's monetary policies may be important beyond simply maintaining an equilibrium exchange rate between them. *To stabilize their common price level, the symmetry of the situation suggests that, institutional arrangements being equivalent, the supply of one country's money should fall by as much as that of the other increases.*

If only A's central bank were active in the foreign exchanges so that M_a fell with no offsetting expansion in M_b, our two-country world would experience an unexpected net deflation—even though S remained stable. Such unfortunate asymmetry between the United States and other industrial countries in the 1970s and 1980s is examined in chapter 4.

ANNEX • WHY STERILIZED INTERVENTION IS NOT ENOUGH

Out of concern for national monetary independence, recent theorizing (Henderson 1982, Dornbusch 1982) emphasizes the efficacy of *sterilized intervention* in response to sudden shifts in international *bond* portfolios: the exchange rate is stabilized but the domestic money supply is left unchanged. At most, this view could be appropriate for an insular economy, but is invalid for one that is financially open.

Consider our previous example of an open economy starting in full financial and trade equilibrium, when suddenly a political event occurs that makes the election of a future left wing government more likely. Nervous international investors try to dump domestic bonds in favor of foreign bonds and cause an (incipient) depreciation of the domestic currency. Prevailing theory then suggests that this precipitate shift in portfolio preferences should be sterilized, i.e., prevented from changing any nominal domestic price such as the interest or exchange rate.

How is sterilization implemented? To stabilize the exchange rate, the central bank initially draws down its foreign exchange reserves (foreign bonds) and buys domestic money—thus causing a (transitory) fall in the domestic money supply. Then, to prevent the domestic interest rate from increasing, the central bank immediately undertakes an open market operation to buy domestic bonds and pump domestic money back into circulation. The upshot of this sterilized intervention is that the private stock of domestic bonds falls and the stock of foreign bonds rises—while interest rates, the exchange rate, and the stock of domestic money remain unchanged.

In open economies without exchange controls, what is wrong with this plausible line of reasoning favoring sterilized intervention as the primary technique for stabilizing the exchange rate? If investors want more foreign bonds and fewer domestic bonds because of the political scare, why not accommodate them?

First, successful sterilized intervention is often *not feasible* because of the lack of any complementary interest rate adjustments. Official exchange intervention would need to be of the same order of magnitude as the ex ante shift between privately held domestic and foreign bonds. However, official reserves remain small relative to the huge outstanding stocks of private financial assets. A sterilized official response to a significant shift in private portfolio preferences lacks credibility, and could quickly lead to an overwhelming loss of reserves.

For example, on August 1, 1983, the US Treasury announced that the governments of the United States, Germany, and Japan had "launched a coordinated exchange market intervention to stem the rise of the dollar and calm disorderly foreign exchange markets" (*Wall Street Journal*, 2 August 1983). But without further monetary action, this tripartite intervention and its announcement effect quickly washed out. By January 1984, the dollar had risen much further against European currencies. In the turbulent 1970s and 1980s, many similar ineffectual official exchange market interventions—without supporting changes in national monetary policy—have been tried.

Secondly, the theory favoring sterilized intervention is based on an *incorrect empirical presumption:* that major shifts in preferences between domestic and foreign bonds are arbitrary or unwarranted. The resulting exchange rate fluctuations are simply a (serious) nuisance that should be sterilized lest they infect an otherwise healthy and stable domestic economy. But because in practice virtually all such changes in international portfolio preferences reflect reasonable shifts in peoples' risk assessments about the future of the open domestic economy, interest rates and monetary policy should respond to pressure in the foreign exchanges—as we have just shown.

The one clea, case where sterilized intervention is both necessary and effective is when exchange controls hamper movements of private capital as if the economy were insular, and a current account deficit or surplus develops. Then the government itself must become an international financial intermediary (McKinnon 1980). In the case of a current surplus with upward pressure on the exchange rate, the government should intervene to buy foreign bonds and sell domestic bonds—sterilized intervention—in order to replace the (artificially) restricted outflow of private capital.

4 How the Dollar Exchange Rate And Foreign Money Growth Affect The American Economy

For the 1971–83 period of volatile exchange rates and extensive official exchange intervention (in dollars) by foreign central banks, how did international influences impinge on US prices and GNP? The theoretical analysis in chapter 3 suggests that pressure on the exchange rate should unambiguously indicate expected changes in the supply of, or effective demand for, domestic money. In this chapter, I show that the dollar depreciations of 1971–73 and 1977–78, and the great dollar appreciation of 1981–83 (figure 1.1) did indeed telegraph the future course of American inflation or deflation. The dollar exchange rate turns out to be a robust leading indicator of fluctuations in American GNP and in the dollar prices of internationally tradable goods.

But, at the center of the world dollar standard, the United States is not just a typical open economy. Foreign central banks in other industrial countries usually intervene to smooth the wilder fluctuations in their dollar exchange rates. Consequently, their domestic money growth tends to vary *inversely* with the strength of the dollar in the foreign exchanges, as shown below, and thus magnify worldwide cyclical fluctuations. The second part of this chapter statistically analyzes how fluctuations in "world" money provide potentially useful signals on the future course of the American (and world) business cycle—beyond that information contained in the dollar exchange rate itself.

The Weakening Relationship Between US Money And Nominal GNP

Let us put foreign money growth to one side for now, and consider the United States as a "small" open economy facing a relatively stable outside world. How can changes in the US money supply be disentangled from changes in US money demand[1] in their impact on American nominal GNP?

---

1. Notice that the demand for money can change through indirect currency substitution (changing international risk premia on domestic interest rates) even though the domestic demand-for-money function is stable. Therefore, the conventional econometric approach, of testing for the stability of the demand-for-money function, is of limited usefulness.

Consider the money supply side first because it is directly observable. Table 4.1 provides annual percentage growth rates of US M1—coin and currency and checking deposits—for 1956 through 1983 as prepared by the Federal Reserve Bank of St. Louis.[2] Except possibly for 1983 itself, American money growth has been considerably smoother than that of other countries since 1970, and even smoother (albeit higher) than US money growth back in the 1950s and 1960s when exchange rates were fixed. Floating rates seem to have given the United States more monetary autonomy on the supply side, as conventional theory suggests.

Table 4.2 displays annual growth in *nominal* US GNP from 1958 to 1983. Since 1971, growth in nominal GNP has been generally higher: greater price inflation more than offset lower real growth. However, I shall not try to distinguish fluctuations in real output from changes in the GNP price deflator. The model presented here only purports to "explain" fluctuations in nominal GNP.

Consider now a single regression equation linking nominal American GNP—as denoted by Y^{US}—to current and lagged values of American M1—denoted by M^{US}.

(4.1) $\dot{Y}^{US} = C + a\dot{M}^{US} + a_{-1}\dot{M}^{US}_{-1} + a_{-2}\dot{M}^{US}_{-2} + u$

The dot over each variable represents percentage rates of change; no subscript indicates that the variable is current, whereas $\dot{M}_{-2}$ is money growth with a one-year lag, $\dot{M}_{-2}$ has a two-year lag, and so on. C is just a constant (which could be related to the trend in velocity), and the "a" coefficients measure the strength of each of the lagged money supply variables. The sum of the a's is important for the overall impact of money supply changes on nominal GNP.[3] Equation (4.1) is one representation of "domestic monetar-

---

2. The average money stock is computed over each calendar year, and then annual percentage changes are taken in these averages and reported in table 4.1. If, instead, percentage changes were based on point estimates of the money stock on the last day of each year, the resulting statistical series of money growth would be much less stable.

3. In my econometric analysis, the signs of the a's are not constrained to be positive. More conventionally, money growth is often measured by three- or four-year moving averages, or other similarly common statistical procedures designed to ensure that the a's are always positive. Unfortunately, such standard smoothing techniques are not appropriate for measuring business cycles of one to three years' duration. A natural but disconcerting consequence of my using linear regression analysis to measure cyclical effects in GNP is the pattern of positive and negative signs on the money supply variables in the fitted equations shown in appendix C.

ism'': the widely held view that instability in GNP is primarily due to fluctuations in the supply of money under the presumption that the demand for domestic money is relatively stable.

The random variable or "disturbance," u, signifies that equation (4.1) is just a statistical relationship where the independent variables in the right-hand side need not fully explain all the variance in the dependent variable on the left-hand side. Table 4.3 summarizes the results from fitting equation (4.1) by the method of ordinary least squares for two economically different time intervals: the 1958–69 period of fixed exchange rates, and the 1972–83 period of dirty floating. This partitioning of the data can be further justified statistically. As measured by a conventional "F" test, the regression coefficients in the earlier period differ significantly from the later period. (These regression results are reported more fully in tables C-1 and C-2 of appendix C.)

By common convention, $\bar{R}^2$ measures the percentage of variance explained in the left-hand variable of fitted regression equations such as (4.1). For 1958–69, US money growth explains 63 percent of the variance in American GNP growth as measured by the $\bar{R}^2$ shown in table 4.3. Then $\bar{R}^2$ falls to .33 in 1972–82. (Remember, the maximum value for $\bar{R}^2$ is 1.0.)

If very preliminary estimates for nominal GNP and nominal money growth for 1983 are incorporated, the explanatory power of equation (4.1) disappears altogether for the 1972–83 period. $\bar{R}^2$ is not significantly different from zero in the regression of GNP on money for 1972–83—as shown in table 4.3. This decline in explanatory power of US M1 accords with the general view of financial commentators: the (lagged) velocity of money in recent years has become increasingly unstable—especially in comparison to the 1950s and 1960s.

Some readers might be (rightly) suspicious of the arbitrary lag structure employed for the money supply variables in equation (4.1). In table C-2 of appendix C, the analysis is repeated using 6-month and 18-month lags for the money supply variables (instead of one- and two-year lags). Although qualitatively the same, the results are even stronger, as shown in the upper panel of table 4.3. The attempt to explain fluctuations in nominal US GNP by US money alone works well in the 1950s and 1960s when exchange rates were fixed but becomes progressively weaker in the period of floating exchange rates. In the early 1980s, this decline in the statistical power of a pure money supply equation is particularly sharp.

What was the proximate cause of the deterioration in statistical fit in the last couple of years? The comparatively low annual growth in nominal GNP

TABLE 4.1   **Money growth in domestic currencies, 11 industrial countries (percentage change in annual averages of M1)**

	Belgium	Canada	France	Germany	Italy	Japan
(Weights: GNP 1964)	(.0132)	(.0394)	(.0778)	(.0892)	(.0494)	(.0681)
1956	2.9	-1.2	10.3	7.2	8.5	16.4
1957	-0.1	4.0	8.6	12.1	6.3	4.1
1958	5.8	12.8	6.4	13.1	9.9	12.8
1959	3.2	-3.2	11.4	11.8	14.0	16.5
1960	1.9	5.1	13.0	6.8	13.5	19.1
1961	7.7	12.4	15.5	14.8	15.7	19.0
1962	7.2	3.3	18.1	6.6	18.6	17.1
1963	9.8	5.9	16.7	7.4	16.9	26.3
1964	5.6	5.1	10.3	8.3	6.7	16.8
1965	7.4	6.3	9.0	8.9	13.4	16.8
1966	6.7	7.0	8.9	4.5	15.1	16.3
1967	4.7	9.5	6.2	3.3	13.6	13.4
1968	6.8	4.4	5.5	7.6	13.4	14.6
1969	2.3	6.9	6.1	8.2	15.0	18.4
1970	-2.5	2.4	-1.3	6.4	21.7	18.3
(Weights: GNP 1977)	(.0172)	(.0487)	(.0885)	(.1122)	(.0471)	(.1404)
1971	10.3	12.7	13.7	12.0	22.9	25.5
1972	15.0	14.3	13.0	13.6	18.0	22.0
1973	9.8	14.5	9.9	5.8	21.1	26.2
1974	6.8	9.3	12.6	6.0	16.6	13.1
1975	12.4	13.8	9.9	13.8	8.3	10.3
1976	9.6	8.0	15.0	10.4	20.5	14.2
1977	8.0	8.4	7.5	8.3	19.8	7.0
1978	6.7	10.0	11.2	13.4	23.7	10.8
1979	3.5	6.9	12.2	7.4	23.9	9.9
1980	-0.2	6.3	8.0	2.4	15.9	0.8
1981	3.6	4.3	12.3	1.2	11.1	3.7
1982	3.4	2.0	14.9	3.5	9.9	7.1
1983	—	—	—	—	—	—

—Not available.
Source: Federal Reserve Bank of St. Louis, "International Economic Conditions," June and August 1983.

TABLE 4.1   **(Continued)**

Nether- lands	Sweden	Switzer- land	United Kingdom	United States	World average	Rest of world[a]
(.0144)	(.0167)	(.0113)	(.0796)	(.5408)		
−3.7	7.4	6.0	1.0	1.1	3.78	6.94
−2.0	3.4	1.8	2.7	−0.6	2.43	6.01
11.9	1.6	9.2	3.0	4.3	6.47	9.04
4.5	18.0	6.1	4.6	0.1	4.53	9.74
6.7	−1.2	10.2	−0.8	−0.4	3.72	8.58
7.7	10.7	8.1	3.2	2.9	7.39	12.68
7.5	5.6	16.6	4.4	2.1	6.18	10.99
9.8	8.1	8.9	0.3	2.8	6.86	11.65
8.5	7.7	0.2	5.0	4.1	6.16	8.59
10.9	6.4	12.8	2.7	4.3`	6.59	9.30
7.2	9.9	3.1	2.6	4.6	6.31	8.33
7.0	9.8	6.0	3.2	3.9	5.49	7.37
8.8	−1.8	11.5	6.0	7.0	7.51	8.12
9.4	2.0	9.5	0.4	5.9	7.00	8.30
10.6	7.3	9.8	6.4	3.8	5.80	8.15
(.0228)	(.0195)	(.0148)	(.0572)	(.4316)		
16.7	9.0	18.2	11.8	6.8	12.45	16.74
17.7	11.8	13.4	13.1	7.1	12.21	16.10
7.4	9.6	−1.0	8.6	7.3	11.06	13.91
3.1	16.3	−1.7	4.8	5.0	7.78	9.88
18.7	15.2	2.4	15.6	4.7	8.83	11.96
11.8	14.0	7.3	13.8	5.7	9.91	13.10
14.3	8.3	4.7	14.4	7.6	8.72	9.57
5.3	13.6	12.7	20.1	8.2	10.99	13.11
2.7	12.7	7.8	11.5	7.7	9.23	10.39
4.2	21.1	−5.4	4.9	6.2	5.53	5.01
2.6	12.0	−0.9	10.0	7.2	6.50	5.96
4.9	9.8	3.1	8.3	6.5	6.96	7.31
—	—	—	—	11.2[b]	—	—

a. United States excluded.
b. Preliminary data.

40   AN INTERNATIONAL STANDARD FOR MONETARY STABILIZATION

TABLE 4.2   **Growth in nominal income, 11 industrial countries (percentage change in annual GNPs)**

	Belgium	Canada	France	Germany	Italy	Japan
(Weights: GNP 1964)	(.0132)	(.0394)	(.0778)	(.0892)	(.0494)	(.0681)
1958	0.8	3.8	14.9	7.2	7.4	4.0
1959	3.1	6.0	9.8	8.8	6.3	12.2
1960	6.5	4.1	11.0	18.6	15.7	19.8
1961	5.9	3.4	9.0	10.0	11.2	23.5
1962	6.9	8.3	11.8	8.3	12.3	10.9
1963	7.4	7.1	12.1	6.0	14.5	15.4
1964	11.8	9.4	10.9	9.8	9.5	18.1
1965	9.1	10.1	8.5	9.2	7.6	12.9
1966	7.4	11.7	7.4	6.4	8.4	16.2
1967	7.1	7.4	8.0	1.3	10.2	17.2
1968	7.1	9.3	8.7	8.4	8.4	18.5
1969	10.9	10.0	14.0	11.7	10.4	17.7
1970	11.4	7.4	11.7	13.6	12.5	17.9
(Weights: GNP 1977)	(.0172)	(.0487)	(.0885)	(.1122)	(.0471)	(.1404)
1971	9.3	10.2	11.5	11.3	8.9	10.1
1972	12.0	11.4	12.4	9.4	9.7	14.6
1973	13.3	17.4	13.6	11.2	19.5	21.8
1974	17.4	19.4	14.7	7.3	23.4	19.1
1975	10.6	12.1	13.6	4.9	13.2	10.4
1976	13.7	15.5	15.5	8.7	24.9	12.1
1977	8.0	9.3	12.3	6.7	21.3	11.3
1978	7.4	10.3	13.6	7.5	16.9	9.9
1979	6.2	13.7	13.9	8.3	21.3	8.0
1980	6.4	10.6	13.0	6.7	25.1	7.3
1981	3.4	13.3	11.9	4.0	17.6	6.5
1982	7.7	5.3	14.6	3.6	16.8	5.1
1983	—	—	—	—	—	—

—Not available.
Source: See table 4.1.
a. United States excluded.
b. Preliminary data.

TABLE 4.2 (*Continued*)

Nether-lands	Sweden	Switzer-land	United Kingdom	United States	World average	Rest of world[a]
(.0144)	(.0167)	(.0113)	(.0796)	(.5408)		
1.6	5.6	2.8	4.3	1.3	3.79	6.73
7.0	6.4	6.4	5.1	8.5	8.25	7.95
11.2	8.9	10.1	5.9	3.8	7.83	12.59
4.9	8.8	12.3	6.8	3.6	6.80	10.57
7.1	8.5	10.9	5.0	7.7	8.36	9.13
8.9	7.2	9.6	6.4	5.6	7.51	9.77
17.6	11.5	10.9	9.2	6.9	8.98	11.44
11.5	10.0	7.2	7.5	8.4	8.81	9.29
8.6	8.8	7.7	6.7	9.4	9.20	8.96
10.0	8.5	7.6	5.6	5.8	6.75	7.88
10.4	6.1	7.4	8.0	9.2	9.51	9.87
13.4	8.6	8.5	7.5	8.1	9.80	11.80
12.3	12.0	11.8	9.7	5.2	8.50	12.38
(.0228)	(.0195)	(.0148)	(.0572)	(.4316)		
13.0	8.5	13.4	12.3	8.6	9.86	10.81
13.4	9.5	13.1	10.7	10.1	11.08	11.82
14.9	11.3	11.6	15.1	11.8	14.20	16.03
13.2	13.1	8.9	13.8	8.1	12.12	15.17
9.0	17.4	−1.3	26.2	8.0	10.08	11.67
15.0	12.9	1.8	18.8	10.9	12.61	13.91
14.5	8.5	3.2	15.4	11.7	11.45	11.34
7.7	11.4	3.7	14.6	12.8	11.50	10.82
5.9	12.1	4.9	16.6	11.7	11.63	11.36
5.8	13.4	7.1	17.1	8.9	10.01	10.93
4.3	8.3	9.7	10.4	11.6	9.82	8.61
4.6	8.3	5.7	9.1	4.1	6.28	7.94
—	—	—	—	7.7[b]	—	—

TABLE 4.3   Regressions for US nominal GNP:[a] percentage of variance explained

$$(0 \leq \overline{R}^2 \leq 1)$$

Explanatory variables (percentage change)	1958–69	1972–82	1972–83
US money supply only			
Lagged by calendar years	0.63	0.33	0.00[b]
6- and 18-month lags	0.80	0.50	0.02[b]
US money supply and dollar exchange rate[c]			
Lagged by calendar years	n.a.	0.89	0.57[b]
6- and 18-month lags[d]	n.a.	0.86	0.78[b]

n.a. Not applicable for the 1950s and 1960s when the dollar exchange rate did not fluctuate significantly.

Source: See appendix C. These are the best fits—highest $\overline{R}^2$—for each lag structure. The best fit is with the exchange rate lagged only one year, and the money supply lagged at most two years.

a. Annual percentage changes in American gross national product as presented in table 4.2.

b. Based on preliminary 1983 data.

c. Based IMF dollar exchange rate trade weighted against 17 industrial countries—see lower panel of figure 1.1

d. Money supply lagged 6 and 18 months, with the exchange rate on a one-year lag.

in 1982 and 1983—of 4.1 percent and 7.7 percent, respectively (table 4.2)—occurred despite the fact that money growth did not fall in 1982 or 1983 below its norms for the 1970s. Indeed, the 11.2 percent growth in M^{US} from 1982 to 1983 was very robust by the standards of the 1970s (table 4.1). The domestic monetarist model would have predicted higher growth in nominal GNP than what was actually observed.

My simple single equation estimating procedure, based on 11 or 12 annual observations, need not be the best measure of the impact of US money on US nominal GNP. It is unduly sensitive to the addition of one more observation: witness the sharp further decline in the goodness of fit when the preliminary 1983 observation was added. Elaborate multi-equation statistical models based on quarterly or monthly observations—taking into account levels as well as rates of growth in the variables—might give a better fit. Nevertheless, domestic money growth *by itself* no longer seems adequate to explain cyclical fluctuations in nominal GNP growth.[4] In a financial sense, the open American economy of the 1970s and 1980s appears quite different from its more insular counterpart of the 1950s and 1960s.

The Dollar Exchange Rate and American Nominal GNP

Alternatively, suppose that shifts in the (indirect) demand for US money have become more important in the 1970s and 1980s compared to the two preceding decades. Under floating exchange rates, international investors continually move from financial assets denominated in one currency to those denominated in another. Although remaining very important, the effects of money supply changes by themselves could then be obscured—as reflected in the poor statistical fit for equation (4.1).

Consider amending our basic regression equation to include the dollar exchange rate as an additional explanatory variable incorporating "news" that reflects these demand shifts—as explained in chapter 3.

$$(4.2) \quad \dot{Y}^{US} = C + a\dot{M}^{US} + a_{-1}\dot{M}^{US}_{-1} + b\dot{E} + b_{-1}\dot{E}_{-1} + u$$

$\dot{E}$ is the annual percentage change in the International Monetary Fund's measure of the dollar exchange rate—trade-weighted against 17 other industrial countries as shown in the lower panel of figure 1.1. Because E is measured in foreign currency units per dollar, $\dot{E}$ being positive reflects dollar appreciation—and vice versa. The "a" coefficients still represent the impact of money supply changes on nominal GNP, whereas the "b" coefficients reflect the impact of fluctuations in the exchange rate. Equation (4.2) thereby permits supply side and demand side fluctuations to be distinguished from one another.

From fitting equation (4.2) for the period of floating from 1972 to 1983, changes in the dollar exchange rate appear to have a major impact on GNP growth within a year or so. That is, the b_{-1} coefficient in equation (4.2) is

---

4. It remains true, of course, that countries such as Portugal and Italy with high trend rates of growth in their money supplies will have higher trend rates of price inflation than hard currency countries such as Germany and Japan.

negative and highly significant at the 95 percent level of confidence or better.[5] Taking our lowest numerical estimate of $b_{-1} = -0.26$ to illustrate, if the dollar exchange rate appreciates by 10 percent this year, growth in nominal GNP slows down by 2.6 percentage points next year—for any given time path in the US money supply.

Consider the same important phenomenon from a slightly different viewpoint. $\bar{R}^2$ increases as one moves from fitting equation (4.1) with the money supply only, to equation (4.2) where the exchange rate is also included as an explanatory variable. The relevant comparisons are set out in table 4.3. In the last two columns for 1972–82 and for 1972–83, one can see the sharp increase in $\bar{R}^2$ in moving from the upper panel (money supply only) to the lower panel (money supply and exchange rate). The proportion of total GNP variance explained by our regression equation increases sharply when the exchange rate is included.

This statistical result is at least consistent with the hypothesis that fluctuations are dominated by shifts in the effective demand for US money, as analyzed in chapter 3. In the early 1980s, for example, the appreciating dollar clearly signaled that the international (indirect) demand for base money in the United States had unexpectedly risen. The stance of monetary policy was unduly tight although money growth in 1980–82 was no less than usual—and from 1982 to 1983 was considerably higher than the average of the past dozen years (table 4.1). Thus the exchange rate picked up the great deflation of the early 1980s, just as it had earlier signaled the two great inflations of the 1970s. And this shows up as a higher $\bar{R}^2$ in the lower panel of table 4.3.

Although the exchange rate is a good indicator of deflation (or inflation) to come, it is also partly the instrument by which deflation (or inflation) is effected. The increased demand for dollar assets in the early 1980s drove the dollar up in the foreign exchanges and directly depressed the American tradable goods industries. Exports fell and imports increased.

But dollar appreciation also signaled Americans that expected price inflation would be even lower than they had previously thought. Consequently, US portfolio preferences shifted away from goods and real estate and back into financial (dollar) assets. This signaling effect from dollar appreciation

---

5. Using different lag structures for both $\dot{M}^{US}$ and $\dot{E}$ as shown in tables C-1 and C-2 in the statistical appendix, b_{-1} varies within a range of -0.26 to -0.30 for the regression based on the 1972–82 interval. The numerical values for b_{-1} become considerably higher, between -0.30 and -0.35, when the preliminary 1983 data are included.

contributed to an additional deflationary impact within the American economy—even in those sectors not directly touched by foreign trade.

The statistical significance of the money supply variables is enhanced once the exchange rate is included in the regression. In equation (4.2) money growth has a positive effect on GNP in the near term—within a year or so—but has a more negative effect when longer lags are taken into account (appendix tables C-1 and C-2). This part of my analysis fits with the conventional monetarist wisdom that control over the domestic money supply remains important.

If the exchange rate alone is used to explain American nominal GNP, the statistical fit is very poor. Without the money supply as a complementary explanatory variable, the impact of the exchange rate on nominal GNP is obscured. This tends to confirm the monetary approach in which the exchange rate reflects shifts in effective money demand, rather than the narrower interpretation: that it is some exogenous nonmonetary force acting only on imports and exports.

In short, in order to measure either supply side or demand side monetary influences properly, separate indicators (explanatory variables) for each need to be incorporated into the statistical estimating procedure.

However, our econometric procedure is confined to measuring *changes* in the dollar exchange rate from one year to the next, as shown in figure 1.1. *Sustained* overvaluation or undervaluation of the dollar—measured from some purchasing power parity—is not captured.

Only when floating is "clean," moreover, can the dollar exchange rate fully reflect changes in US money demand arising from disturbances in the international bond market. Massive interventions by foreign central banks somewhat dampened those fluctuations actually observed. Hence, by no means all relevant information on shifting international currency preferences is captured by our exchange rate series. Much scope remains for refining the econometrics beyond the simple technique embedded in equation (4.2).

Monetary Repercussions in Other Industrial Countries

Let us now drop our simplifying assumption that the United States is a "small" open economy because it is the center of the world dollar standard. Shifts in the demand for dollar assets have a substantial impact on money growth in other industrial countries—Japan, Canada, and those of Western Europe. And from our principle of indirect currency substitution, we suspect that these currencies are somewhat substitutable with each other in determining inflation or deflation in the world at large.

The money supplies, whose rates of change appear in table 4.1, are defined narrowly to include currency and checking accounts in the M1 category for each of the 11 countries. Precisely which of these convertible currencies are the strongest substitutes for each other, and which should enter with the heaviest weights in any index of world money, is not addressed. The international moneyness of, say, the German mark, is not distinguished from that of the Italian lira. Nevertheless, table 4.1 includes the principal monies that are used to invoice world trade and to denominate internationally liquid wealth in the Euromarkets. In short, we are interested in a narrow definition of money in the spectrum of financial assets, but one which has effective potential as an international medium of exchange and standard of value.[6]

In table 4.1 "world" money growth, the aggregate for these 11 industrial economies as a group, is compiled as the weighted sum of percentage growth rates in national monies *without* adjusting for exchange rate fluctuations. From 1956 to 1970, the fixed weights are relative GNPs in the year 1964 for which the US enters with a weight of .5408. From 1971 through 1982, the United States receives a lower weight of .4316 based on GNPs in 1977. The right-hand column shows money growth in the rest of the world (ROW, 10 industrial countries with the United States excluded) also on the basis of these fixed GNP weights.

Why do other industrial countries individually have wider fluctuations in money growth than the United States since floating began? Foreign central banks (weakly) pursued exchange rate targets while the Fed did not. The impact of such interventions on their domestic monetary bases often could not be sterilized, causing the erratic patterns seen in table 4.1. For example, the variable pattern of M1 growth in Germany and Switzerland in recent years belies their contention that they are following the principle of constant growth in domestic money.

Consider now aggregate money growth for these industrial countries as a group as shown in table 4.1. During the 1950s and 1960s, world money

---

6. Eurocurrency deposits per se are omitted because they are more like bonds than money, important though these interbank deposits may be for linking national capital markets and providing a channel for indirect currency substitution. Eurocurrency deposits are not checking accounts used by nonbanks as a means of payment.

growth (inclusive of the United States) was smoother than American money growth itself. Fluctuations in national money growth rates tended to offset each other under the fixed exchange rate regime.

After 1970, however, table 4.1 shows that world money growth becomes more episodic and cyclical. Modest fluctuations in American money growth were *magnified* by monetary fluctuations in ROW. This greater instability in world money growth is related to the breakdown of the fixed exchange rate regime. Any (modest) acceleration of American money growth heightens expectations of higher US inflation. International investors then are more apt to switch out of dollars in the absence of any firm dollar exchange parities. Foreign central banks are unwilling to let the resulting dollar appreciation go too far; they eventually intervene to buy dollars and sell their own currencies, causing their domestic money supplies to increase. Since 1970, the three great swings in the dollar exchange rate (figure 1.1) were accompanied by major changes in world money growth (table 4.1).

Even if American money growth were stable, political events could cause a flight from (or into) dollars with similar consequences. In retrospect, one can hardly distinguish shifts in US money growth, initiating a flight from dollars, from "pure" demand shifts in portfolio preferences against dollar bonds due to some exogenous political or economic news. "Nonmonetary" disturbances were present in each of the three major changes in international portfolio preferences for dollar assets. Let us discuss each in turn.

THE DOLLAR DEPRECIATION OF 1971–73

Although American money growth increased from its average of the 1960s, the breakdown of the Bretton Woods system of dollar parities was engineered by the American government's trying to force a dollar devaluation. In August 1971, President Nixon permanently closed the US Treasury's gold window to foreign central banks and imposed a temporary import surcharge until dollar parities were finally realigned in the Smithsonian Agreement of December 1971. In response to threatened devaluation throughout 1971, international investors moved out of dollar assets. The Smithsonian dollar parities broke down in late 1972 and early 1973. Nevertheless, the vain attempt of foreign central banks to maintain these dollar exchange parities— see their sharp 1971–72 build-up of dollar exchange reserves in table 1.1— led to the explosive growth in ROW money shown in table 4.1.

THE DOLLAR DEPRECIATION OF 1977-78

Again mild expansion in the rate of US money growth (table 4.1) was accompanied by attempts—beginning in early 1977—of US officials (including the Treasury secretary) to "talk" the dollar down. This news interacted with uncertainty about the appointment of a new chairman for the Federal Reserve Board of Governors, and what the future course of American monetary policy might be. The result was akin to an inflation scare that induced international investors to shift out of dollar assets into European currencies and the Japanese yen. The resulting dollar depreciation—almost 35 percent against yen and marks over two years (figure 1.2)—again induced foreign central banks to intervene to buy dollars. Table 1.1 shows the increase in their dollar reserves in 1977-78. Table 4.1 shows another increase in world money growth in 1978—although not as massive as in 1971-73. Despite the absence of official dollar parities, the behavior of foreign central banks was qualitatively the same in the second period as the first. Instability in world money growth, emanating from the United States, was magnified.

THE DOLLAR APPRECIATION OF 1981-82

In October 1979 the Federal Reserve system abandoned short-term interest rates as a monetary indicator, which indeed had contributed to the loss of monetary control in the two earlier episodes. With the avowed aim of disinflating the American economy, the Fed adopted a stricter monetarist growth rule. From table 4.1, one can see the modest decline in annual US money growth from about 7.6 percent over 1977-79 to about 6.5 percent in 1980-82.[7] Throughout late 1979 and the first two-thirds of 1980, however, the market remained unconvinced that the Fed would stick with its disinflation. Then a series of "accidental" political shocks occurred, which dramatically changed international portfolio preferences toward dollars:

- By mid-1980, the anticipated election of a more conservative American president. Although the Fed's disinflation policy remained unchanged, people began to believe that it would be brought to a successful conclusion.

---

7. One could justifiably argue that US money growth decelerated more sharply because of financial innovation: the rapid growth in interest-bearing checking accounts in the latter period. This complication does not affect my main argument.

- Political turmoil in Europe in 1980–81: the threat of Russian military intervention in Poland, a socialist government in France imposing a wealth tax and tighter exchange controls, and financial crises in several European countries.

- An unbalanced financial liberalization in Japan: by the end of 1980 exchange controls on international capital flows had been removed while the Bank of Japan continued managing some yen interest rates at below market levels—much as the American government had regulated US bank deposits in the 1970s.

- By 1982, a huge US fiscal deficit emerged—not financed by additional money issue—which caused high real rates of interest in the United States.

The upshot of these accidental political events was a sharp increase in the demand for dollar assets, a great appreciation of the dollar with exchange rate "overshooting," and—beginning in 1980—the precipitate fall in ROW money growth (shown in table 4.1) as foreign central banks tried to prevent an undue depreciation of their currencies. What began as disinflation in the United States turned into the worldwide economic slump of 1981–82. In effect, there had been a big increase in the derived demand for US base money which—being on a monetarist rule—the Fed did not then accommodate. (Subsequently, Fed policy became much more expansionary from mid-1982 throughout 1983.)

The International Money Multiplier

Suppose each of our 11 countries' money growth was independently determined as under a "clean" float. Then the statistical law of large numbers would suggest that proportional variance in world money should—on average—be *less* than that for important individual countries. How then can one succinctly characterize why the supply of "world" money (inclusive of US M1) has been *more* unstable than money growth in the center country itself?

The interventions of foreign central banks were *passively sterilized* by the Fed, i.e., they did not have any effect on the US money supply. Under the institutions of the world dollar standard, foreign interventions in the exchange markets did not directly touch the American monetary base. If the deutsche mark came under sudden downward pressure, the Bundesbank would draw down its reserves of US Treasury bonds (table 1.1) to repurchase DM base money. The German money supply would contract—as it did in 1981 (table

4.1)—but the American money supply would not expand in an offsetting fashion. Only the stock of US Treasury bonds owned by the private sector would increase—not the American monetary base itself.[8] This asymmetrical arrangement made it particularly easy for the Fed to ignore the foreign exchanges in order to focus on domestic monetary indicators such as US interest rates or growth in US M1.

Under such a regime of passive sterilization by the center country, any *autonomous* money growth by the United States—say, by a domestic open market operation—will force an *even greater expansion in world money* (Swoboda 1978) if other countries intervene to forestall their currencies from appreciating unduly. Through this international money multiplier, therefore, the relatively mild fluctuations in US money growth further aggravated the variance in world money—even when international portfolio preferences remained stable on the demand side.[9]

Both these demand side and supply side disturbances in world money were correlated with observed movements in the dollar exchange rate. When the dollar was weak, foreign money usually grew above its norm and vice versa. Consequently, in our regression equation (4.2), part of the strong impact of the dollar exchange rate on US nominal GNP reflected repercussions from fluctuations in the rest of the world's money supply.[10] This is an important channel through which the US business cycle becomes worldwide—with unfortunate reinforcing feedback effects on the American economy itself.

To be sure, exchange rate changes may insulate other industrial countries from international cycles of economic activity. For example, the undervalued yen in 1981–82 helped the Japanese avoid as sharp a setback in industrial output as occurred in the United States. By allowing its currency to appreciate sharply in 1978–79, Germay managed to avoid high American-level price inflatión in 1979–80 (see table 4.4). But on balance, the world is thrown into depression when the dollar becomes strong and growth in (world money)

8. The annex to chapter 5 shows how these institutional arrangements could be altered to yield a more symmetrical monetary adjustment between the United States and other hard currency countries.

9. For a complete algebraic development of how these demand side and supply side disturbances work themselves out under passive sterilization, see McKinnon (1982).

10. In single equation statistical regressions, changes in ROW money growth (unadjusted for exchange rate fluctuations) turn out not to be directly useful in explaining fluctuations in US nominal GNP. See the critical comment by Radcliffe, Warga, and Willet (1983), and the reply by McKinnon and Tan (1983). As shown below, however, ROW money is useful in explaining prices of US tradable goods.

contracts, and the global economy experiences an inflationary boom when the dollar becomes weak and world money increases. However, the distribution of this worldwide inflationary (deflationary) pressure depends on the relative over- and undervaluation of each industrial country's exchange rate.

Imagine a two-stage inflation process in a world where national monies are somewhat substitutable in demand for each other. First, growth in the aggregate money stock determines the overall inflationary pressure in the system. Secondly, countries whose currencies are relatively overvalued will experience little price inflation compared to those that are undervalued.

The International Burden of Dollar Indebtedness

There is another important channel by which fluctuations in the dollar exchange rate—magnified by monetary fluctuations in other industrial countries—exacerbate the international business cycle. In the Third World, import expenditures by both governments and private entities are severely constrained by their heavy foreign indebtedness in dollars. Consequently, when the dollar appreciates against European or Japanese currencies where LDCs sell their exports, and appreciates against the prices of internationally tradable goods—particularly price-sensitive primary commodities—their debt-service payments in dollars become much harder to meet. LDCs are, therefore, forced to curtail expenditures in world markets in general and for American goods in particular.

The reverse was generally true in the 1970s with dollar depreciation and unexpected inflation in the dollar prices of internationally tradable goods. The wealth or "budget" constraint on LDC spending in the world economy was (artificially) relaxed, and reinforced the inflationary boom.[11]

But what about dollar creditors in the industrial world? Shouldn't they experience an offsetting improvement in their wealth position and undertake increased expenditures when the dollar appreciates? Generally speaking, no.

First, insofar as dollar creditors reside in the private sector of the United States, their wealth as measured in dollars (their operational numeraire) does not increase when the dollar appreciates against other currencies. Americans didn't feel wealthier in the sense of wanting to increase their expenditures for commodities.

---

11. The same story can be told slightly differently. LDCs faced a decrease in the real—inflation adjusted—interest rate when the dollar depreciated. Correspondingly, the "real" interest rate on their outstanding debts increased sharply when the dollar appreciated in the early 1980s (Cline 1983).

Secondly, Steven Ambler (1983) has shown that the private sectors of other industrial countries are, on balance, neither significant dollar creditors nor dollar debtors. However, *governments* in other industrial countries are big dollar creditors because of their holdings of US Treasury bonds and bills. But these creditor governments don't typically adjust their current spending for goods and services to changes in their net international asset position— as long as their exchange reserves are above some minimal level of adequacy.

Consequently, when the dollar appreciates, no positive wealth effect in the industrial countries including the United States offsets the increased burden of dollar indebtedness in LDCs. The international demand for goods and services falls. Some of the feedback effects on the United States of this debt-burden effect are also picked up in the regression coefficient for the dollar exchange rate in equation (4.2).

In contrast, suppose one ignored the operations of the dollar standard, and built a model of the world economy that treated the United States symmetrically with other countries or blocs of similar size. Then, if the dollar unexpectedly became overvalued and the currency of the other bloc became undervalued, there would be no presumption of *net* inflationary or deflationary pressure in the world overall. Deflationary pressure in the United States would be balanced by inflationary pressure elsewhere. But this is a world for the academic journals, not the one in which we live.

Price Inflation in Tradable Goods

Equations (4.1) and (4.2) focused on an explanation of domestic nominal GNP in the United States without trying to build a more complex model that would distinguish real output from price-level changes. And that important distinction would be even harder to make for the world economy at large.

However, the hard currency prices of internationally tradable goods are interesting in their own right. Understanding the process of international price inflation is important if any central bank is to stabilize successfully the purchasing power of its own money.

In table 4.4, broad wholesale price indices (WPIs)—inclusive of finished goods and primary products—are a good approximation to tradable goods' prices in the domestic currencies of each of our 11 industrial economies. Let us focus just on two broad measures:

- the American wholesale price index, because so much of world trade is invoiced in dollars

- a "world" wholesale price index over our 11 currencies that encompass all the significant monies used for invoicing international trade.

Table 4.4 shows percentage growth rates in both the American and world WPIs, which are constructed using the same fixed GNP weights as our monetary series in table 4.1. This is clearly shown in figure 4.1.

FIGURE 4.1   **World money supply and US wholesale prices**

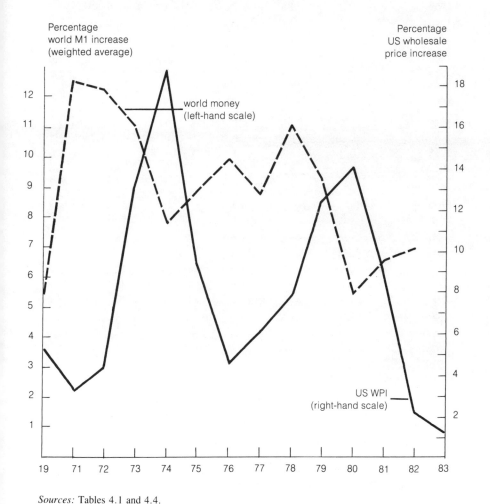

Sources: Tables 4.1 and 4.4.

TABLE 4.4   Price inflation in tradable goods, 11 industrial countries
(percentage change in annual averages of WPIs)

	Belgium	Canada	France	Germany	Italy	Japan
(Weights: GNP 1964)	(.0132)	(.0394)	(.0778)	(.0892)	(.0494)	(.0681)
1958	−4.4	0.4	5.1	−0.5	−1.7	−6.5
1959	−0.3	0.8	7.2	−0.8	−2.9	0.9
1960	1.2	0.2	3.5	1.3	0.8	1.1
1961	−0.2	0.2	3.0	1.5	0.0	1.1
1962	0.8	1.1	0.6	0.9	3.2	−1.6
1963	2.5	1.3	2.9	0.5	5.3	1.6
1964	4.7	0.9	3.5	1.0	3.0	0.4
1965	1.1	1.3	0.7	2.5	1.8	0.7
1966	2.1	2.9	2.8	1.7	1.5	2.4
1967	−0.9	1.9	−0.9	−1.0	−0.2	1.7
1968	0.2	2.2	−1.7	−0.7	0.6	1.0
1969	5.0	3.7	10.7	1.9	3.6	2.0
1970	4.7	2.4	7.5	5.0	7.4	3.7
(Weights: GNP 1977)	(.0172)	(.0487)	(.0885)	(.1122)	(.0471)	(.1404)
1971	−0.5	2.0	2.1	4.3	3.3	−0.8
1972	4.0	4.3	4.7	2.5	4.1	0.8
1973	12.4	11.2	14.7	6.6	17.2	15.8
1974	16.8	19.1	29.1	13.5	40.8	31.4
1975	1.2	11.2	−5.7	4.6	8.5	3.0
1976	7.1	5.1	7.4	3.7	23.8	5.0
1977	2.4	7.9	5.6	2.7	16.6	1.9
1978	−1.9	9.3	4.3	1.2	8.4	−2.5
1979	6.3	14.4	13.3	4.8	15.5	7.3
1980	5.8	13.5	8.8	7.5	20.1	17.8
1981	8.2	10.1	11.0	7.7	16.6	1.7
1982	7.7	6.0	11.1	5.8	13.9	1.8
1983	—	—	—	—	—	—

—Not available.

Source: IMF, *International Financial Statistics, 1982 Yearbook* and August 1983, line 63; wholesale price indices including finished goods and primary products.

TABLE 4.4   *(Continued)*

Nether-lands	Sweden	Switzer-land	United Kingdom	United States	World average	Rest of worlda
(.0144)	(.0167)	(.0113)	(.0796)	(.5408)		
−1.3	4.3	−3.2	0.8	1.5	0.68	−0.30
0.2	0.9	−1.6	0.3	0.2	0.57	1.00
0.0	4.1	0.6	1.3	0.2	0.81	1.54
−0.2	2.2	0.2	2.6	−0.4	0.47	1.50
0.3	4.7	3.3	2.3	0.2	0.64	1.16
2.4	2.9	3.9	1.0	−0.4	0.72	2.03
6.1	3.4	1.3	3.1	0.2	1.15	2.27
3.0	5.2	0.6	3.5	2.0	1.98	1.95
5.0	6.4	1.9	2.9	3.4	3.02	2.57
1.0	4.3	0.3	3.1	0.2	0.45	0.75
1.9	2.0	0.1	4.1	2.4	1.68	0.83
−2.5	3.5	2.8	3.7	3.9	3.99	4.09
4.6	6.8	4.2	7.1	3.6	4.54	5.65
(.0228)	(.0195)	(.0148)	(.0572)	(.4316)		
4.5	3.2	2.1	9.1	3.3	2.94	2.67
5.1	4.6	3.6	5.3	4.4	3.74	3.24
6.9	10.3	10.7	7.4	13.1	12.42	11.91
9.6	25.3	16.2	22.6	18.8	22.00	24.43
6.7	6.4	−2.3	22.2	9.3	6.93	5.12
7.8	9.0	−0.7	17.3	4.6	6.58	8.09
5.8	9.2	0.3	19.8	6.1	6.35	6.55
1.3	7.6	−3.4	9.1	7.8	4.99	2.86
2.7	12.5	3.8	12.2	12.5	10.73	9.39
8.2	13.9	5.1	16.3	14.0	13.33	12.82
9.2	11.6	5.8	10.6	9.0	8.50	8.13
6.6	12.6	2.6	8.6	2.1	4.80	6.85
—	—	—	—	1.3b	—	—

a. United States excluded.
b. Preliminary data.

From the right-hand columns of table 4.4, the great volatility of tradable goods prices in the 1970s and 1980s—compared to the tranquility of the 1950s and 1960s—is immediately evident. Without any formal statistical regression analysis, moreover, the sharp changes in "world" money growth shown in table 4.1 obviously *preceded* the great increases and decreases in the rate of international price inflation shown in table 4.4. In 1971–73 and 1977–78 the two explosions in world money (combined with dollar depreciation) were followed by high worldwide price inflation in 1973–74 and again in 1979–80. Subsequently, the dollar appreciation and the monetary slowdown of 1980–82 were followed by a sharp decline in commodity price inflation in 1982–83. These correlations between world money and American prices are clearly shown in figure 4.1.

Might not the two worldwide price inflations be better explained as oil shocks, courtesy of the Organization of Petroleum Exporting Countries (OPEC), rather than as monetary disturbances? I believe not. World money increased in 1971–72 and early 1973 prior to the Arab-Israeli war in late 1973 that triggered the first oil shock; and increased again in 1977–78 well before the Iranian revolution in 1979, which caused the second oil shock. Because of these prior losses of monetary control, the world was in for two big price inflations whether or not there were specific disturbances in the market for oil. Indeed, OPEC was surprised by bigger price increases than even it anticipated from the production cutbacks in 1973–74 and again in 1979. Of course, OPEC made the two price inflations somewhat bigger than they otherwise would have been.

More than most people realize, however, cyclical fluctuations in the price of oil are endogenously determined by worldwide monetary fluctuations. Under pressure of the great world deflation of 1982–83, OPEC was forced to cut the price of oil from about $34 to $29 per barrel in early 1983. Most cartels in primary products tend to unravel when deflations occur. In practice, of course, "endogenous" fluctuations in oil prices can't be distinguished from those that are "exogenous." Consequently, the price of oil has been left out of my formal statistical analysis to follow.[12]

To explain inflation in the dollar prices of internationally tradable goods as shown in table 4.4, consider the following statistical format:

(4.3) $\dot{P}^{US} = C + a\dot{M}^W + a_{-1}\dot{M}^W_{-1} + a_{-2}\dot{M}^W_{-2} + b_{-1}\dot{E}_{-1} + u.$

---

12. The preliminary evidence suggests that no qualitative change in my conclusions would emerge if the price of oil is somehow included as an additional "exogenous" explanatory variable (Radcliffe, Warga, and Willett 1983b).

Equation (4.3) shows how the regression was run to get the result portrayed in the lowest panel of table 4.5 and in appendix table C-5. $\dot{P}^{US}$ is percentage growth in the US WPI, $\dot{M}^W$ is percentage growth in "world" money as it appears in table 4.1, and $\dot{E}$ is still the percentage change in the effective exchange rate. For the 1972–82 period, table 4.5 tells us that the $\bar{R}^2$ was 0.93. That is, world money and the dollar exchange rate succeeded in explaining 93 percent of the variance in American tradable goods prices over 1972–82. By itself, world money still explained 82 percent of the variance in US wholesale (producer) prices.[13]

Putting the concept of world money to one side, including the dollar exchange rate greatly improves how well US money statistically explains American wholesale prices in the following simple regression format:

$$(4.4) \quad \dot{P}^{US} = C + a_{-1}\dot{M}^{US}_{-1} + a_{-2}\dot{M}^{US}_{-2} + b_{-1}\dot{E}_{-1} + b_{-2}\dot{E}_{-2} + u.$$

In fitting equation (4.4) for 1972–82, table 4.5 shows that $\bar{R}^2$ increases from 0.26 to 0.74 when the exchange rate is included with US money lagged one way, and from 0.37 to 0.82 with a different lag structure. This importance of the dollar exchange rate remains robust when the preliminary 1983 data are included, or when the important mark/dollar exchange rate (not shown) is substituted for the International Monetary Fund's exchange rate index in the regression equations.

Equation (4.4) is written to show the somewhat longer lag structure evident in the regression results found in appendix tables C-3 and C-4. Both money supply and exchange rate changes take somewhat longer to influence US prices than to influence US nominal GNP. Apparently, American monetary disturbances, on either the supply or demand side, affect output first and then prices with a somewhat longer lag.

For the 1972–82 and 1972–83 periods displayed in the middle panels of table 4.5, the dollar exchange rate picks up some of the influence of fluctuations in the omitted world money variable. Similarly, the strong explanatory power of world money by itself for 1972–82 partly reflects the (omitted) dollar exchange rate. The bottom panel suggests that both are important in determining the American price level.

---

13. Other common US price indices, as in the CPI, contain hard-to-measure nontradable services such as medical costs or housing. They are less immediately sensitive to international monetary influences. Nevertheless, inflationary cycles in commodity prices (the WPI) typically lead inflation in other indices. There is a presumption that the central bank should focus on stabilizing some broad commodity price index (McKinnon 1979, ch. 10).

TABLE 4.5   Regressions for prices of US tradable goods:[a] percentage of variance explained

$$(0 \leq \overline{R}^2 \leq 1)$$

Explanatory variables (percentage change)	1958–69	1972–82	1972–83
US money supply only			
Lagged by calendar years	0.43	0.37	0.50[b]
6- and 18-month lags	0.48	0.26	0.37[b]
"World" money supply only			
Lagged by calendar years	0.00	0.82	
US money supply and dollar exchange rate[c]			
Lagged by calendar years	n.a.	0.82	0.84[b]
6- and 18-month lags	n.a.	0.74	0.73[b]
World money supply and dollar exchange rate			
Lagged by calendar years	n.a.	0.93	

n.a. Not applicable for the 1950s and 1960s when the dollar exchange rate did not fluctuate significantly.

Source: See appendix C. These are the best fits—highest $\overline{R}^2$—for each lag structure. The best fit is when the exchange rate and the money supply are lagged at most two years.

a. Annual percentage change in US wholesale price index as presented in table 4.4.

b. Based on preliminary 1983 data.

c. Based on IMF dollar exchange rate trade-weighted against 17 industrial countries—see lower panel of figure 1.1.

d. Money supply lagged 6 and 18 months, with the exchange rate lagged not more than two years.

In contrast, a purely domestic monetary explanation of cyclical price inflation in American tradable goods is becoming progressively less satisfactory. In the upper panel of table 4.5, the explanatory power of US money by itself falls from an $\overline{R}^2$ of 0.48 in 1958–69 to about 0.26 in 1972–82, by one measure.

But this $\overline{R}^2$ statistic somewhat understates the decline in the predictive power of US money. Because absolute price variance was so much higher in the 1972–82 period, that which is *unexplained* by US money rose sharply in comparison to 1958–69. Tables in the statistical appendix provide the standard error of the regression—a measure of the prediction error involved by using US money (without the exchange rate) to predict US prices. This prediction error rose from 1.1 percentage points in 1958–69 (table C-5) to 4.0 percentage points in 1972–82 (table C-3)!

The Recognition Lag in American Monetary Policy: A Concluding Note

What are the policy implications of our statistical analysis? From the 1950s and 1960s to the 1970s and 1980s, the importance of foreign monetary indicators for US monetary policy increased sharply.

In the earlier period, the dollar exchange rate was virtually fixed, and money growth in the rest of the world provided no additional explanation for the US price level. Table 4.5 shows that, in 1958–69, none of the variance in US price was explained by "world" money. Foreign money growth was passively determined within the fixed exchange rate system, and did not reflect major shifts in portfolio preferences for or against dollar assets. Only American monetary policy could independently determine both the American and "world" price levels.[14]

Consequently, in the 1950s and 1960s, American economists—whether they were Keynesians or monetarists—evolved a "closed-economy" view of how best to secure domestic monetary control. The peculiar institutions of the world dollar standard, with convincingly fixed exchange rates, made it easy for the United States—the center country—to vary its domestic money supply while ignoring the foreign exchanges. And, on the whole, this American monetary autonomy was exercised benignly: in the 1950s and throughout most of the 1960s, the dollar prices of international tradable goods remained quite stable (table 4.5).

However, with excessive American monetary (and fiscal) expansion in the late 1960s and early 1970s, the fixed exchange rate system broke down in 1971–73. Equally important, the effective insulation against foreign monetary disturbances that the United States had enjoyed in the earlier era disappeared in more recent times—as demonstrated above.

Unfortunately, in the 1970s and 1980s, prevailing macroeconomic theory continued on its old track of focusing only on domestic monetary indicators as if the United States were an insular economy. Keynesians favored interest

---

14. This important point has been established by Kong-Yam Tan (1984) using more elaborate econometric procedures.

rate targets and monetarists favored stabilizing the growth rate in some purely American monetary aggregate. Because the American government followed prevailing theory(ies) and ignored the foreign exchanges, the American (and world) economy suffered great cyclical instability in the 1970s and 1980s. Unsurprisingly, traditional macroeconomic doctrines fell into disrepute.

Clearly this lag in recognizing the importance of the foreign exchanges for American monetary policy has been very costly. Let us now turn in chapter 5 to how the Federal Reserve System's operating procedures could be explicitly "internationalized" to better stabilize the American economy and those of other countries in the world.

5 A Program for International Monetary Coordination: Germany, Japan, and the United States

To mitigate the cycles of worldwide inflation and deflation characteristic of the past dozen years, the proper coordination of monetary policies has two complementary aspects.

First, in response to continual and unpredictable shifts in international portfolio preferences, nations can adjust their domestic money supplies to stabilize exchange rates. In particular, the United States should alter its long-standing postwar tradition of paying little or no attention to the foreign exchanges in formulating its monetary policy. Orienting national money growth toward the exchange rate can be a powerful instrument for securing exchange stability *and* better balancing the supply of the national money with the direct and indirect demand for it—as demonstrated theoretically in chapter 3. Surprise inflations or deflations that are of a purely national origin would be dampened.

Second, cyclical fluctuations in "world" money—the sum of transactions balances in hard currency countries—must also be avoided. While recognizing the continued resiliency of the American dollar as key currency, the Federal Reserve System needs to make American monetary policy more symmetrical with respect to other important hard currency countries such as Germany and Japan. Instead of being *synchronized* with money growth in the rest of the world (ROW) as was usually the case in the 1970s and early 1980s, US M1 should vary in an *offsetting* fashion through mutual agreement. Growth in world money would then be stabilized.

Securing exchange stability by itself is insufficient if world money is not under control. Conversely, even stable growth in world money could, by itself, still leave unacceptable variance in exchange rates. Under the dollar standard, changes in the dollar exchange rate are particularly upsetting for the American and world economies—as shown empirically in chapter 4. With these constraints in mind, in this chapter I sketch *how* closer cooperation

61

among the central banks of Germany, Japan, and the United States might take place.[1]

Can the Fed Do It Alone?

Consider first the "normal" circumstances where unilateral American action is good enough: when other industrial countries orient their monetary policies toward their dollar exchange rates in a predictable fashion. As demonstrated in chapter 4, the Fed could have mitigated the two great inflationary explosions of the 1970s by contracting the US money supply when the dollar began to weaken and world money growth increased sharply. Similarly, from 1980 to mid-1982, German money growth (and that of other industrial countries) fell sharply as the deutsche mark unexpectedly weakened against the dollar—see table 4.1 and figure 1.2. If, in 1981–82, the Federal Reserve System had expanded the US money supply in an offsetting fashion, the "surprising" worldwide slump of 1982 would have been mitigated. By responding to the (unexpectedly) strengthening dollar and being aware of the shortfall in money growth abroad, the Fed by itself could have prevented the sharp fall in world money growth and undue appreciation of the American currency.[2]

However, monetary events in late 1982 and in 1983 illustrate why a stronger form of monetary coordination might sometimes be necessary. In the late

---

1. Among hard currency countries, the case for monetary coordination and exchange rate stabilization does not depend on close coordination of fiscal policies—other than the commitment of each participating country to maintain price-level stability and not use the inflation tax. Some (preliminary) theoretical arguments are provided in chapter 3 to show that discretionary changes in fiscal policy are less destabilizing when the exchange rate is fixed.

However, this omission of fiscal policy from the mainstream of my analysis does not imply that fiscal policy is unimportant. Even if the exchange rate were stable, large fiscal deficits would cause large trade deficits that generate protectionist pressure. When the United States runs a huge discretionary fiscal (and trade) deficit as in 1983–84, this is a serious savings drain on the world economy, with high interest rates aggravating the debt crisis in the Third World. Unfortunately, monetary policy cannot resolve this serious problem.

2. Because the American government planned for a more gradual disinflation, people were surprised by the sharpness of the 1982 deflation. However, if a rapid reduction of price inflation is deemed preferable to a more gradual approach, the Fed did not err so much ex post facto. Certainly, a rapid return to price stability could, plausibly, be preferable to gradual disinflation—which might be long, uncertain, and drawn out. But for a strategy of draconian deflation to be efficient, i.e., keep losses in real output and turmoil in foreign trade to a minimum, it must be announced in advance and not take everybody by surprise.

summer of 1982, the Federal Reserve's Board of Governors belatedly decided that a more rapid rate of US money growth was imperative. The resulting shift toward monetary expansion was remarkable: from August 1982 to August 1983, US M1 increased about 12.7 percent, and growth in the broader M2 monetary aggregate also increased. The most immediate concern the Fed then faced (and still faces) was the threat of massive default by dollar debtors in Latin America—a threat considerably aggravated by dollar overvaluation. Whatever its real motivation, the Fed subsequently behaved (correctly) as if it were following an exchange rate rule.[3]

Why then in early 1983 didn't the dollar right itself (depreciate) in the foreign exchanges? For once, the European countries did not respond to a strengthening dollar by continued monetary contraction. Having been depressed for so long, the (hard currency) European countries seized the opportunity to expand their money supplies in parallel with the Fed. For example, to the year ended in August 1983, German money growth was about 12 percent—the same order of magnitude as in the United States. Therefore, the dollar did not depreciate against the European bloc. Quite the contrary, figure 1.2 shows that the deutsche mark depreciated further against the dollar in 1983.

However, the Japanese response to continued pressure in the foreign exchanges in favor of the dollar was quite different. The Bank of Japan reduced annual growth in Japanese M1 to about 2.5 percent over the same one-year interval. This induced some significant appreciation of the yen against the dollar from 1982 to 1983 (figure 1.2), which is welcome, and which also led to a larger appreciation of the yen against the deutsche mark— much of which is probably unwarranted. By restraining domestic money growth to (partially) right the yen/dollar exchange rate, Japan played the game correctly over 1983—while the European bloc did not.[4]

---

3. Because of the power of prevailing domestic monetarist ideas, however, this policy switch was not officially rationalized in foreign exchange terms. On October 6, 1982, the Fed announced that the suspension of its M1 target was made necessary by institutional change: the wider introduction of interest-bearing checking accounts that increased the effective demand for M1. Although certainly true, this official explanation cannot explain why growth in the broader US monetary aggregates also increased.

4. However, the Japanese government still regulates yields on domestic bank deposits at below-market levels. Japanese savers still have undue incentive to acquire interest-bearing dollar assets. For strengthening the foreign exchange value of the yen, this regulatory policy remains inconsistent with the Bank of Japan's tight money policy.

What is the general principle involved? The monetary authorities in the hard currency countries should be prepared to deviate symmetrically from their medium-term noninflationary monetary targets so as to allow interest rates, rather than exchange rates, to play a greater role in coping with shifts in international portfolio preferences. Put more simply, this means that money growth in the industrial world should be concentrated in that hard currency country whose currency is unduly strong in the foreign exchanges.

Clearly, the 1983 impasse required an international quid pro quo. The Europeans should have desisted from their rapid money growth *provided that* the Federal Reserve System undertook unusually high money growth in the United States as long as the dollar remains strong and the world economy depressed. Without reaching such an agreement with the Europeans, the Fed was stymied; it could not right the dollar in the foreign exchanges (through US money growth) without running the risk of worldwide price inflation in the future.

Even when American monetary policy is run with a more benign view of the international economy, "dilemma" cases will occasionally arise that are beyond the power of the US government to resolve unilaterally. Acting alone, the Fed might not always be able to stabilize the world (and American) monetary system in an unambiguous fashion.

The Financial Importance of Germany and Japan

Besides the United States, how many other countries need to be brought into a monetary pact for stabilizing the world system? How should one limit the "rest of the world" relevant for reformulating American monetary policy?

From time to time over the past 20 years, one or another of the other 10 currencies portrayed in table 4.1 have been alternatives to the dollar as repositories of international liquidity. Recently, however, some of the major European currencies have become less attractive: British, French, and Italian rates of price inflation (table 4.4) in the last decade have been relatively too high and unstable to satisfy international investors. Reflecting their continuing use of the inflation tax, forcing continual exchange devaluations, Italy and France now impose unusually tight exchange controls on capital account, which makes their monies distinctly less convenient international stores of value.

In contrast, the British financial system was in much better shape by 1983. Inflation had been reduced and exchange controls, limiting British residents' moving between dollar and sterling assets, had been terminated as of 1980.

At the center of the Eurocurrency system and world capital market, Britain is an important financial entrepot in foreign monies.

But sterling itself is no longer much used as an international currency (Bergsten and Williamson 1982). Britain's real economic size is significantly less than the three largest industrial countries—see the relative GNP weights used in table 4.2. And, for technical reasons, the Bank of England does not (chooses not to) exercise direct control over the sterling monetary base—the importance of which will soon become clear. For these somewhat tenuous reasons and for simplicity, I exclude Britain from explicit consideration in the discussion to follow. But the United Kingdom, or other hard currency countries in Europe, could well become part of a more comprehensive agreement.

As of 1984, therefore, the deutsche mark remains the principal "hard" European currency that provides a portfolio alternative to dollar assets. Clustered around Germany are a number of small countries with exchange rates more or less pegged to the DM—and whose monetary policies turn out to be very similar. Indeed, figure 1.2 compares the large fluctuations in dollar/mark exchange rates to the relatively mild movements in Germany's "effective" exchange rate—whose trade weights are dominated by her European trading partners. Within the European Monetary System (EMS), dollar exchange rates of member countries tend to move in concert—except for the occasional negotiated realignment. Let us suppose henceforth that the deutsche mark is "the" European hard currency in international portfolios.

Japan's huge economic size, importance in world trade, and rapid growth make it an obvious candidate for any international pact. Less obviously, the yen is increasingly important as an international currency. Although suffering from very high price inflation in the first monetary explosion of the early 1970s, the purchasing power of the yen has been relatively very stable since the mid-1970s (table 4.4). Over 1978–80, Japan greatly liberalized the detailed exchange controls on capital account that had prevented Tokyo from becoming an international financial center. A further accord to liberalize the remaining restrictions was reached in the US-Japan agreement of November 1983. Foreigners may now hold Japanese financial assets, sell yen-denominated bonds, or borrow directly from Japanese banks. (To be sure, the Bank of Japan still exercises some guidance in these respects.)

Consequently, there has been a marked increase in invoicing of international trade in yen. Euroyen trading is developing more rapidly, and the yen is being used more widely as a standard of value in capital market transactions outside Japan. Central banks in other Pacific Basin countries, such as

Singapore, are increasingly keying on the yen—to some extent supplanting the dollar—as a convenient method of establishing the foreign exchange value of their currencies.

The yen and deutsche mark don't experience the ebb and flow of the demand for dollars fully in concert. One is not entirely representative of the other. The movements in the dollar/yen and dollar/DM exchange rates are related but somewhat differentiated, as shown in figure 1.2. Because of official foreign exchange intervention, both countries have experienced more erratic annual growth in their domestic money supplies (M1) than has the United States. Nevertheless, deviations in the German and Japanese money-growth rates from trend have not been perfectly correlated—as table 4.1 makes clear.

In view of this difference in monetary behavior between Germany and Japan, to what extent is either of their exchange rates representative of the IMF's index for the dollar exchange rate against 17 other currencies? For the 1972–83 period, the statistical regressions (in chapter 4), explaining American tradable goods prices and GNP, work about as well when the bilateral deutsche mark/dollar exchange rate is substituted for the IMF's broader index. The deutsche mark appears to have been the representative alternative foreign asset to the dollar since 1970. The impact of shifts in the mark/dollar exchange rate—or, more accurately, what it indicates for world-wide financial conditions affecting the United States, is strong and sharply focused with about a one-year lag.

In the regression, the yen/dollar exchange rate is neither as good as the IMF's broader exchange rate index nor as the mark/dollar rate. The lagged impact of any change in the yen/dollar rate is less sharply focused and more spread out over the current year and one to two years into the future. Nevertheless, in view of Japan's opening of its domestic capital market to foreigners, and obvious importance in world trade, the yen warrants a greater weight as an international reserve currency then the regression equations, dominated by data from the 1970s, might suggest.

In summary, while both the deutsche mark and yen are important reserve currencies and potential alternatives to the dollar, each should be recognized as an independent entity in any international monetary pact. Harmonized monetary relationships among the triumvirate—Germany, Japan, and the United States—should go a long way toward stabilizing the international monetary system as a whole. No other substantial sources of "world" money for invoicing foreign trade or international financial transactions are in prospect.

Targeting Growth in World Money

Independently of any exchange rate mechanism, the three countries need to reduce fluctuations in their combined money supply—narrowly defined to be the means of payment used by nonbank firms and individuals. Therefore a target for joint money growth, based on normal money growth in each of our three countries, can be introduced *before* specifying some method of varying money supplies in each country to secure better exchange stability. Controlling growth in world money is necessary in order to stabilize the joint price level.

Start from the proposition that percentage growth in the nominal money stocks, taken to be M1 or narrow transactions balances, of each of our three countries should enter with a fixed weight in determining percentage growth in world money. Suppose further that this weighting system is independent of any arbitrary starting set of exchange rates linking the three currencies, and independent of any subsequent or actual exchange rate changes. Then, our international rule is of the form:

$$(5.1) \quad \dot{M}^W = .45\dot{M}^{US} + .35\dot{M}^{GE} + .20\dot{M}^{JA}$$

where a dot ($\cdot$) over a variable denotes percentage change on an annual basis. M^W is the relevant world money stock, and the other superscripts refer to the United States, Germany, and Japan, whose money supplies are measured in dollars, deutsche marks, and yen respectively.

The substantial but merely illustrative weight of 0.35 assigned to Germany reflects its disproportionate importance in the European Monetary System. Taking Germany to represent "Europe," these numerical weights are very similar to those that the International Monetary Fund uses in defining its unit of account, i.e., Special Drawing Rights. That is, the United States gets about 45 percent of the weight and Japan gets 20 percent. In practice the exact weighting system would be negotiated by the three central banks, taking financial importance and the relative size of GNPs into account. (The rate of growth in the broader definition of world money in table 4.1 is calculated in a similar fashion.)

The preferred procedure is to calculate individual growth rates for M1-type transactions balances for the United States, Germany, and Japan on a monthly basis, and to instruct the three participating central banks to aim for annual growth in this sum, $\dot{M}^W$, of, say, 6 percent.[5] For example, a target range for $\dot{M}^W$ of 5 percent to 7 percent for the following year could be jointly agreed on. Six percent is our hypothetical estimate of that growth in "world" money, which would stabilize the "world" price level: the weighted index of tradable goods prices across our three countries—similar to but narrower than the 11-country index shown in table 4.4.

Normal Money Growth and Tradable Goods Prices

How then should this aggregate money growth be allocated among our three countries?

Consider first the "normal" pattern of money growth, supposing that the three economies start in monetary balance: *no* exchange rate disequilibrium or price-level misalignment across countries. The "world" price level is itself stable. Each country's projected money growth would be designed to maintain long-run price stability in a similar broad basket of *tradable goods*.

In practice, this implies near zero inflation in each country's wholesale price index (WPI) rather than in the consumer price index (CPI) or in the GNP deflator. Both of the latter price indices have important nontradable components. With a stable WPI as the target, and in the absence of portfolio disturbances, each country's domestic money growth is then consistent with long-run exchange rate stability.

These normal money growth rates depend on some estimate of future growth in real GNP, trends in velocity, and on an allowance for growth in the prices of nontradable goods and services. Generally speaking, a high-growth economy like Japan, where increases in productivity are greatest in the tradables sector, will experience a higher rate of price inflation in the nontradables components of GNP than will a slower growing economy like the United States. (Japan's CPI tends to increase secularly relative to its WPI.) Therefore Japan needs to be assigned a somewhat higher long-run rate of domestic money growth than projected "real" GNP might indicate. (If

5. From equation (5.1), $\dot{M}^W$, the percentage growth in world money, is a well-defined monetary indicator easily calculated from the sum of our three national money growth rates, $\dot{M}^{US}$, $\dot{M}^{GE}$, and $\dot{M}^J$. I have yet to define the absolute magnitude of M^W itself. Indeed the reader or central bankers following equation (5.1) need never know the precise definition of M^W. This rule governing percentage growth in world money, $\dot{M}^W$, would still be fully operational. To asuage intellectual curiosity, however, what M^W itself means, in terms of the units in which it might be measured, is discussed more fully in appendix B.

Japan did try to stabilize its CPI, this would be inconsistent with long-run stability in the yen/dollar exchange rate.)

Elsewhere (McKinnon 1979, ch. 10), I have explained somewhat more fully how these calculations could be made. To avoid misplaced concreteness and excessive detail in the present context, however, let us simply presume that normal, or long-run, money growth in each country is known. Such growth rates are not far from what a domestic monetarist, with a wholly insular view of his economy, might prescribe.

For example, suppose this long-run money growth is 5.5 percent in both the United States and Germany and 8 percent in Japan. Ongoing money-supply operations in each country are then oriented to these targets. These illustrative growth rates in M1-type transactions balances have been chosen so that, if money growth is so sustained in each country, growth in M^W would be exactly 6 percent when each of the national money growth rates is weighted according to equation (5.1). Of course this is within our hypothetical target range of 5 percent to 7 percent.

Because these *long-run* money supply targets are compatible with zero secular inflation in each country's tradable goods prices, exchange rates would exhibit no short-run tendency to change in one direction or the other without some portfolio disturbance on the demand side. Such pressure in the foreign exchanges would signal each central bank to vary its current money supply to accommodate this demand shift. The simplest and least structured format for any tripartite monetary agreement then suggests itself:

Each central bank would deviate from normal money growth according to whether its currency was strong or weak in the foreign exchanges. These deviations in national money growth rates would be subject to the constraint that world money be kept within its target range. If one central bank is substantially above its normal money growth path, at least one other should be symmetrically below.

From our previous empirical analysis, the demand for world money—the joint money supply of the three reserve-currency countries—is more stable than the demand for any one of them. And this remains true in the absence of exchange controls or other undesirable impediments to international capital flows.

Exchange Rate Alignment in Stage One

Consider "Stage One" of a new tripartite monetary agreement that comes into existence when price levels are not necessarily aligned, nor are they stable. In such a disequilibrium state, how could the monetary authorities begin the process of coordination?

After a dozen years of unexpectedly large exchange rate movements, and diverse changes in national price levels, "equilibrium" nominal exchange rates can hardly be calculated with any precision in 1984. Neither is massive official intervention in the foreign exchanges warranted in order to precipitate any *discrete* exchange rate corrections. Instead, the system should simply be nudged back in the direction of exchange equilibrium.

In Stage One, we assume that the three financial systems can't be unified overnight, equalizing interest rates as complete exchange stability would require. However, the triumvirate can still move with dispatch in jointly controlling world money, i.e., preventing synchronized money growth in Germany and Japan that effectively magnifies monetary fluctuations in the United States. The cycle of inflation and deflation that has characterized the world economy of the past dozen years—associated with the ebb and flow of speculation against the American dollar—could be successfully tamed even as major exchange rate fluctuations are subdued.

Beginning in a state of exchange rate disequilibrium, the key operational problem is one of assigning short-run monetary growth (deviations from normal growth) according to which country's currency is undervalued and which is overvalued. Hence the problem of calculating rough "equilibrium" exchange rates cannot be avoided. What are the principles involved?

Prices and costs in domestic commodity markets—largely those in the diversified manufacturing sector—should be kept aligned across the three countries. Applying this principle requires some purchasing power parity (PPP) calculation: selecting an appropriate base year and price or cost indices for deflating subsequent changes in nominal exchange rates. In the technical appendix, I outline one such calculation of the "real" yen/dollar and deutsche mark/dollar exchange rates using 1975 as the base year and changes in unit labor costs for deflating nominal exchange rate movements. Remembering that the margin for error is large, the results are reproduced in table 5.1.

Throughout 1983 and into early 1984, the rates of internal price inflation within Germany, Japan, and the United States have converged to a very low level. Hence the PPP exchange rates of 210 yen per dollar and 2.0 deutsche marks per dollar held approximately for any month or day during 1983 or early 1984.

To check on the robustness of these PPP calculations, I compare them to John Williamson's estimates of equilibrium exchange rates calculated in much more complex fashion. Table 5.1 shows Williamson's "Fundamental

TABLE 5.1   **Real and nominal dollar exchange rates: Germany and Japan**

	Yen	Deutsche mark
Purchasing power parity[a]	210	2.00
Upper margin limit	220	2.10
Lower margin limit	200	1.90
Actual rate as of September 12, 1983	243	2.63
Williamson[b] calculation of the "Fundamental Equilibrium Rate" for September 1983	205	2.04
Actual rates as of February 10, 1984	234	2.73

a. These calculations are taken from the technical appendix and are based on unit labor costs with 1975 chosen as the base year. In 1983 or early 1984, Ұ210 and DM2.00 are the values that the yen/dollar and deutsche mark/dollar exchange rates would have to assume if purchasing power parity was correctly established.

b. John Williamson, *The Exchange Rate System*, POLICY ANALYSES IN INTERNATIONAL ECONOMICS 5 (Washington: Institute for International Economics, September 1983).

Equilibrium Exchange Rates" for September 1983 of Ұ205 and DM 2.04. His point estimates fall well within a moderate 10 percent band of Ұ200 to Ұ220, and of DM 1.9 to DM 2.1, around my PPP exchange rates.

Accepting these or similar calculations, suppose the three central banks agree among themselves in Stage One to establish soft target zones—ones they are not immediately obligated to achieve—for their exchange rates. By adjusting domestic money growth, in 1984 they begin nudging their dollar exchange rates toward, say, Ұ220 and DM 2.1, subject to the important constraint that joint money growth remains under control. No sudden direct intervention in the foreign exchanges would be contemplated; neither would discrete domestic monetary adjustments be undertaken. Rather, in 1984, the Federal Reserve System would push American money growth above its norm of 5.5 percent per year, whereas the Bundesbank and Bank of Japan would have money growth substantially below their norms of 5.5 and 8.0 percent, respectively.

If the dollar were to suddenly fall below these rough exchange rate targets, then this monetary machinery would be thrown into reverse. Money growth in the United States would be reduced below its long-run norm, while monetary policies in Germany and Japan would become more expansive.

With this idealized monetary regime in place, trade deficits or surpluses will frequently appear. They simply reflect the balance between saving and investment, i.e., between income and expenditures, in each country and with the outside world. As shown in chapters 2 and 3, once the exchange rate is stable and national money supplies vary symmetrically to maintain it, private capital flows will automatically finance trade deficits or surpluses. Consequently, our three central banks need not—had best not—negotiate over what trade balances are "appropriate."

If one country, say the United States in 1983–84, begins to run an abnormally large fiscal deficit, the natural consequence will be a very large trade deficit even if the *nominal* exchange rate was close to its "correct" PPP level. High expenditures relative to output in the United States would undoubtedly cause imports to increase relative to exports. Because of the fiscal deficit, a large American trade deficit becomes inevitable no matter how exchange rates are established.

From our analysis in chapter 3, however, only modest changes in the real exchange rate are a necessary adjunct to substantial changes in the trade balance, and these are often best secured over months or years through *gradual* changes in the prices of nontradables. As the fiscal (and trade) deficit develops, the nominal exchange rate is best kept constant—or within very narrow bounds—in order to insulate domestic industries producing tradable goods from some precipitate change in the economy's international competitiveness. Monetary policy is effectively subordinated to aligning national price levels and stabilizing the purchasing power of each country's money—and would not be geared to "correcting" trade imbalances.

For implementing international monetary coordination, the minimal format described above—Stage One—is undemanding in several important respects:

● New exchange parities within narrow margins are not required. The three central banks need only respond to gross exchange rate misalignments.

● How each national money supply is altered from its norm is unspecified. Domestic open market operations or unsterilized intervention in the foreign exchanges could be used.

● How Germany and Japan might best manage their dollar exchange reserves—with possible implications for each monetary base—is left open.

● Preexisting monetary agreements or exchange rate pacts, such as Germany's membership in the European Monetary System, are not contravened.

Although representing an important conceptual change in the way each of the three central banks operates, Stage One need not require new legislation or major institutional changes in the operating procedures of each of the three participating central banks.

Announcing the New Policy

Suppose the three central banks agree among themselves to something similar to Stage One. The question then inevitably arises: to what extent should the new system be publicized?

At the very minimum, each central bank—but particularly the Fed with no recent historical precedents in this matter—should state that the foreign exchanges are now receiving substantial weight in determining monthly or quarterly money growth rates. But long-run "norms" for domestic money growth in each country are still being retained. Without some such explanation, financial markets will be unnecessarily upset.

For example, if domestic money growth is more than they anticipated, monetarist gnomes may surmise that the authorities have thrown away the rulebook and are on another inflationary binge; or, they may anticipate a sharp monetary contraction in the immediate future. Either surmise would cause unnecessary interest and exchange rate volatility. However, once the central bank explains its general orientation toward exchange stabilization, and the domestic currency has obviously been strong in the foreign exchanges, then everybody can sit back and relax. Indeed, American financial gnomes (other than domestic monetarists) would feel quite comfortable when they knew the Fed was committed to contracting the American money supply if the dollar fell too far, or too precipitately.

An eminent British journalist, Samuel Brittan, has kindly volunteered what the Fed's spokesman should say:

"In fixing its short-term monetary growth objectives, the Fed now intends to take into account the overseas as well as the domestic demand for dollars . . . When the dollar was particularly strong against other currencies, the money supply target would be increased; when it was weak the target would be reduced." (*Financial Times*, 12 July 1982).

In Stage One, whether or not the three central banks should specifically publicize their target zones for exchange rates is more questionable— particularly since there is no fixed timetable for getting there. If domestic price levels are not moving in concert (unlike 1983), the zones themselves would have to be continually recalculated. When monetary coordination is just getting underway, perhaps publicizing firm estimates of exchange rate targets would be unwise.

However, when each central bank announced "interim" money growth rates from time to time, the market could infer in what direction the authorities were trying to nudge their exchange rates. For example, after suspending its M1 target for some months after October 1982, in July 1983 the Fed decided on a 6 percent to 9 percent range for M1. Because the dollar remained strong in the foreign exchanges, and this growth rate was higher than any long-run noninflationary norm, the market could infer that the Fed thought that the dollar exchange rate was too high. Monetary expansion is quite safe provided that foreign money growth is under proper control.

Such a system, where central banks take the foreign exchanges into account but do not publish a specific exchange rate zone, would be robust in an informational sense. If some newspaper purloined the secret minutes revealing the current (soft) exchange rate targets of the triumvirate, no panic would result. On balance, however, when exchange rates are far out of alignment the official target is best not publicized lest the authorities seem rigidly committed to it.

Suppose, however, that substantial progress is made to align exchange rates within the target zones, and the three central banks convince themselves that their techniques of monetary coordination are adequate. The triumvirate may then be more forthcoming in describing their target zones for the yen/dollar and mark/dollar exchange rates, and their interim target for joint money growth. Because by then the financial markets would likely have already divined all that, such revelations would be anticlimactic.

By this advanced stage, just announcement effects by themselves would have a powerful impact on keeping exchange rates within the desired narrow range. Actual monetary policy in each country would not need to change much—relative to normal growth—to secure this result. Stabilizing expectations by private traders would be quite dominant.

Fixed Exchange Rates in Stage Two: A Concluding Note

Some readers may be willing to accept Stage One without wanting to go further. Exchange rates are kept within fairly broad target zones determined by purchasing power parity or the Williamson alternative, and the system is anchored by joint control over the supply of yen, deutsche marks, and dollars. But no substantial direct official intervention in the foreign exchange is mandated. Had it been in place, Stage One itself would have mitigated the gross exchange rate misalignments, and cyclical fluctuations in prices and incomes, experienced by the industrial world in the past dozen years.

Yet, if Stage One is successfully introduced, a strong case can be made for going on to Stage Two: more complete financial unification among the reserve currency countries. Instead of adjusting purchasing power parities continually, nominal exchange rates would be fixed within narrow hard margins—such as the 2 percent band specified in the original Bretton Woods agreement. In Stage Two official intervention in the foreign exchanges would be designed to eliminate short-run exchange and interest rate *volatility* for any one country, to equalize interest rates across countries, and to fully stabilize a broad index of internationally tradable goods prices.

How financial policies could be coordinated in Stage Two requires much more detailed planning, outlined in the annex to this chapter. However, because potential financial unification is some years away, keeping Stage Two tucked away in the annex seems appropriate. Fortunately, the case for proceeding with Stage One is compelling whether or not Stage Two is ever seriously considered.

Suppose Germany, Japan, and the United States progress in harmonizing their monetary policies in the 1980s. The yen/dollar and mark/dollar exchange rates are stabilized, as is the price level for tradable goods measured in any of these three currencies. Then, in order more easily to establish the purchasing power of their own monies, governments in smaller countries will voluntarily peg to one of the three. The international monetary system would devolve to the comparative tranquility of the Bretton Woods era of the 1950s and 1960s.

The international cycle of inflation and deflation—through uncontrolled changes in world money and the dollar exchange rate—would be smoothed. The efficiency of international trade should be restored and protectionist sentiment should diminish once arbitrary changes in exchange rates are eliminated. As in an idealized gold-standard regime, domestic and international money would become virtually the same.

But unlike a gold standard, which would be hostage to convertibility crises and vagaries in the aggregate gold base of participating countries, the monetary base of the new international standard would be under the joint control of the Bundesbank, the Bank of Japan, and the Federal Reserve System. And unlike the postwar dollar standard under either fixed or floating exchange rates, the United States would cede some autonomy in determining the supply of dollars in order better to stabilize the demand for them.

ANNEX • MONETARY CONTROL UNDER FIXED EXCHANGE RATES

In Stage Two, nominal exchange rates would be fixed within narrow margins. The Bundesbank and Bank of Japan would announce new dollar parities, say DM 2.0 and ¥210, maintained within 1 percent margins—DM 1.98 to DM 2.02 and ¥208 to ¥212—by direct official intervention. Inside these margins, commercial banks would remain responsible for clearing all international payments across currencies. In contrast to the original Bretton Woods system, however, control over aggregate money growth would be jointly exercised by the three countries—as described above.

Of course, such a fixed rate system—Stage Two—should be adopted only once Stage One was seen to be successful: nominal exchange rates had been kept within broad target zones for some years through the successful coordination of national monetary policies. Only after substantial time had elapsed at virtually stable exchange rates and domestic price levels, could the authorities convince themselves that existing exchange rates were in "equilibrium," and could be safely fixed.

Why go to fixed exchange rates in Stage Two if much of the gain from stabilizing the international economy is already achieved in Stage One?

First, the commitment to an *international* monetary standard of stable purchasing power is politically important. Whether or not to debase the domestic currency is taken out of the immediate realm of domestic politics in each country—as with the protection of civil liberties under the judicial system today or the operation of the gold standard in the nineteenth century.

To complement this political argument, I have demonstrated that national monetary stability cannot be successfully pursued unilaterally within any economy open to international shifts in portfolio preferences. If nations don't hang together, they may hang separately. In effect, the political ramifications of such an international monetary pact are similar to a strong form of the General Agreement on Tariffs and Trade (GATT)—a reciprocal international agreement that exercises a substantial restraining influence on the domestic economic policy of each participating country.

In a world with fixed exchange rates and stable prices, the GATT would itself become stronger. Monetary stability increases the potential for securing free trade, and unhindered international commodity arbitrage undermines domestic monopolies by making it more difficult for interest groups to push prices or wages above market-clearing levels. Price-level stability is easier to maintain.

Second, there is a more purely financial argument why stable exchange rates within narrow hard margins are likely to be advantageous. Floating exchanges rates have been characterized by a high degree of volatility on a day-to-day or week-to-week basis. Interest rates have also become more volatile since 1970—particularly in the United States since October 1979 when the Fed (correctly) had to give up pegging the short-term rate on federal funds. If by continual intervention in the foreign exchanges, each government succeeds in better balancing the supply of and demand for the domestic currency, both interest rate and exchange rate volatility would diminish. Financial perturbations—often associated with the movement from one money to another—would abate. (Obviously, this argument requires a great deal more empirical and analytical support before most readers will be comfortable with it.)

Assuming Stage Two is desirable, what further provisions—beyond those already agreed to in Stage One—are necessary? The main technical problem in Stage Two is to define precisely how official intervention in the foreign exchanges should best take place. Remembering that alternative strategies are conceivable, consider the following set of rules which would do the trick.

● Recognizing the existing exchange intervention practices under the dollar standard, the Bundesbank and Bank of Japan would have the primary responsibility for direct intervention—whereas the Federal Reserve system would stay passive on a day-to-day or week-to-week basis.

● Neither German nor Japanese interventions would be sterilized in their domestic monetary consequences.

● Symmetrically, when official intervention occurs, the Fed would allow its monetary base to change in the direction opposite to that of the other two countries. To ensure that this American response was automatic, the Bundesbank and Bank of Japan would hold their working exchange reserves directly on deposit with the Federal Reserve Bank of New York (at a market rate of interest).

In effect, each of the three countries would divide its monetary base into a *domestic* and a *foreign* component. The domestic component would grow according to a prespecified rule so as to achieve the long-run money growth targets, i.e., 5.5 percent in Germany and the United States, and 8 percent in Japan. Open-market operations in domestic currency bonds would be the principal instrument for achieving this steady growth in the domestic component of the base. In contrast, the foreign component of each country's monetary base would vary with the ebb and flow of the international demand for each currency—as accommodated by official intervention to stabilize the two exchange rates.

Stripped to essentials, the foreign and domestic components of each country's monetary base are represented by the balance sheets of the three central banks as they appear in table 5.2. For each country, A represents the

TABLE 5.2   **Foreign and domestic components of the monetary base: the United States, Germany, and Japan**

Federal Reserve System (dollars)

Domestic assets: government bonds and loans to commercial banks	A^{US}	MB^{US}	American monetary base: currency *plus* reserves of US commercial banks
		FR^{GE}	Deposits of Bundesbank
		FR^{JA}	Deposits of Bank of Japan

Bundesbank (deutsche marks)

Domestic assets	A^{GE}	MB^{GE}	German monetary base: currency *plus* reserves of German commercial banks
Foreign reserves held with the Fed	FR^{GE}/S^{GE}		

Bank of Japan (yen)

Domestic assets	A^{JA}	MB^{JA}	Japanese monetary base: currency *plus* reserves of Japanese commercial banks
Foreign reserves held with the Fed	FR^{JA}/S^{JA}		

Note: S^{GE} is the average historical exchange rate for dollars/deutsche marks, whereas S^{JA} is the average historical exchange rate for dollars/yen. Thus, current or future exchange rate fluctuations would have no direct effect on the German or Japanese monetary bases.

domestic component of its monetary base; FR—deposits of the Bundesbank or Bank of Japan with the Fed—represent the foreign component. For example, when FR^{GE} increases because the Bundesbank buys dollars in the foreign exchanges (all else constant), the German monetary base (MB^{GE}) increases and the American monetary base (MB^{US}) declines. Monetary symmetry is thereby built into the format by which dollar exchange reserves are held.

Sterilization of the monetary consequences of these foreign exchange transactions could not occur as long as domestic assets of each central bank are on a prespecified growth path. Similarly, world money growth is stable because domestic credit expansion is thus restrained.

Because Stage Two is not imminent, it would be misplaced concreteness to provide additional technical details on reserve holdings and exchange interventions. However, two additional major conceptual problems should be mentioned.

First, some broad mutual constraint should be negotiated on the use of fiscal policy: preferably a balanced budget rule for each country over some four- or six-year moving average. Because fixed exchange rates establish a degree of monetary unity, central banks in any one country shouldn't be put in the position of financing fiscal deficits elsewhere. One government should not be able to drain savings from the system on a massive scale and generally increase interest rates—as American fiscal policy is doing in 1983–84. Because the monetary pact is meant to include only "hard" currency countries, fiscal restraint is necessary to discourage any one of them from using the inflation tax in the future—which, of course, is inconsistent with the very idea of fixed exchange rates.

Secondly, provision must be made to tailor "world" money growth to secure full stability in the prices of tradable goods. Much statistical work would have to be done in constructing mutually agreeable price indices for tradable goods, the stability of which is the ultimate target of the monetary triumvirate.

One should consider growth in world money as an interim target for achieving full price-level stability. If internationally tradable commodities— with prices of auction-market goods providing an early warning signal— tended to fall collectively, aggregate money growth should be increased beyond our tentative 6 percent norm. The very success of Stages One or Two might increase the effective global demand for the three currencies, and thus impose an unexpected deflation on the system. Conversely, joint money growth should be slowed if commodity price inflation is threatened. The three central banks should thus stand ready to offset any such changes in the aggregate demand for money.

Once the "big three" had stabilized monetary relations among themselves, other countries would fix their own exchange rates—likely to the dollar, if outside the European Monetary System. However, the exchange reserves of other nations would continue to be held in nonmonetary dollar assets—largely US Treasury bills and bonds. Shifts in the exchange reserve positions of countries not party to the formal monetary agreement would not affect the monetary base of the United States or those of Germany and Japan.

Hence, the joint monetary policy of the triumvirate would be quite autonomous vis-à-vis the rest of the world. It would be similar to that of the United States by itself under the strong dollar standard of the 1950s and 1960s—except that a commitment to smooth growth in the collective monetary base would replace the gold-dollar convertibility constraint of those early postwar years.*

---

* This case for joint monetary control by the triumvirate, to replace the United States' acting by itself, was made by Ronald I. McKinnon in *A New Tripartite Monetary Agreement or a Limping Dollar Standard?*, Essays in International Finance.

Appendix A   Calculating Equilibrium Exchange Rates for Stage One

The illustrative equilibrium exchange rates for 1983, shown in table 5.1, were calculated according to the principle of purchasing power parity—the methodology of which is outlined below.

Choosing a base year when the foreign exchanges are thought to be in equilibrium is somewhat arbitrary, although necessary for tracing subsequent changes in the real exchange rate. In tables A-1 and A-2, 1975 was chosen to be the base year. The nominal yen/dollar and mark/dollar exchange rates were fairly stable in 1975–76, interest rates were fairly well aligned, and rates of price inflation were moderate and quite similar across the three countries. After the breakdown of the Bretton Woods system of fixed exchange rates in 1971–73, and the first oil shock in 1973–74, relative price and cost relationships appeared to settle down in 1975–76. Because some economists believed that the dollar was then overvalued, 1975–76 is a conservative base from which to measure today's dollar overvaluation.

From 1975 to 1982, wholesale prices rose about 72 percent in the United States, 36 percent in Japan, and 38 percent in Germany—see tables A-1 and A-2. Consumer price indices show the same relative divergence. Only in 1983 and early 1984 have the three countries converged to the same absolute rate of inflation—close to zero. But the cumulative impact of the higher American inflation since 1976, combined with the sharp appreciation of the dollar in 1981–83, have left both the yen and the mark undervalued.

THE YEN/DOLLAR RATE

No single price or cost index is likely to provide an adequate explanation of misalignment in real exchange rates, and some perspective on historical trends is important in judging any current measure of the real exchange rate.

In comparing Japan to the United States in table A-1, pure price indices alone don't reveal too much. With 1975 = 100, deflating the nominal yen/

TABLE A-1   The real exchange rate: Japan and the United States
(1975 = 100)

	(1)	(2)	(3)	(4)	(5)	(6)	(7)
	¥/ dollar	¥/ dollar (1975 =100)	Wholesale price indices		Real exchange rate (2/3÷4)	United labor cost	
			Japan	United States		Japan	United States
1960	359.9	121.3	56.1	54.3	117.4	41	70
1965	361.5	121.8	57.3	55.2	117.3	50	67
1970	358.2	120.7	63.8	63.1	119.4	52	79
1975	296.8	100.0	100.0	100.0	100.0	100	100
1976	296.6	99.9	105.0	104.6	99.5	100	102
1977	268.5	90.5	107.0	111.0	93.9	104	108
1978	210.4	70.9	104.2	119.7	81.4	102	114
1979	219.1	73.9	111.9	134.7	88.8	99	122
1980	226.8	76.4	131.7	153.6	89.1	100	137
1981	220.5	74.3	133.6	167.5	93.2	104	146
1982	249.1	83.9	136.0	171.1	105.6	112	159
1982							
Oct	271.1	91.3	137.5	171.1	113.6	116	160
Nov	265.1	89.3	137.2	171.8	111.8	113	160
Dec	242.5	81.7	135.2	171.9	102.3	115	161
1983							
Jan	232.9	78.5	134.1	171.6	100.5	115	161
Feb	236.2	79.6	134.2	172.2	102.1	116	161
Mar	238.0	80.2	133.7	171.9	103.1	114	160
Apr	237.7	80.1	132.8	172.0	103.7	115	159
May	234.8	79.1	132.4	172.5	103.1	113	159
June	240.1	80.9	132.8	173.0	105.4	112	158
July	240.5	81.0	133.1	173.5	105.6	113	156
Aug	244.3	82.3	132.8	174.4	108.1	111	155
Sept	242.8	81.8	132.9	174.7	107.5	111	155
Oct	233.0	78.5	132.0	175.2	104.2	111[a]	154
Nov	235.3	79.3	132.1	174.8	104.9	—	—

— Not available.
Sources: See table A-2.
a. Preliminary data.

TABLE A-1   *(Continued)*

(8) Comparative costs (6/7)	(9) Real exchange rate (2/8)	(10) Wages in manufacturing Japan	(11) Wages in manufacturing United States	(12) Comparative wages (10/11)	(13) Consumer price indices Japan	(14) Consumer price indices United States
.586	207.1	13.6	47	.289	33.2	55.0
.746	163.2	22.0	54	.407	44.5	58.6
.658	183.4	43.7	70	.624	58.0	72.1
1.000	100.0	100.0	100	1.000	100.0	100.0
.989	100.2	112.3	108	1.040	109.3	105.8
.963	94.0	121.9	118	1.033	118.1	112.7
.895	79.2	129.1	128	1.009	122.6	121.2
.811	90.0	138.5	139	.996	127.0	134.9
.730	104.7	148.8	151	.985	137.2	153.1
.712	104.3	157.2	165	.953	143.9	169.0
.704	119.1	164.8	176	.936	147.7	179.4
.725	125.9	166.2	177	.939	150.6	182.4
.706	126.4	166.2	178	.934	148.9	182.1
.714	114.4	167.6	180	.931	148.7	181.4
.714	109.9	167.7	180	.932	149.0	181.9
.720	110.5	168.6	181	.931	148.4	181.9
.713	112.6	170.6	181	.943	149.4	182.0
.723	110.7	170.6	182	.937	149.9	183.2
.711	111.3	166.5	182	.915	151.6	184.3
.709	114.1	174.7	182	.960	150.5	184.9
.724	111.8	174.7	183	.955	149.8	185.7
.716	114.9	173.8	183	.950	149.4	186.3
.716	114.2	174.9	184	.951	151.3	187.2
.720[a]	109.0[a]	176.2	—	—	152.7	187.6
—	—	—	—	—	—	—

TABLE A-2   The real exchange rate: Germany and the United States
(1975 = 100)

	(1)	(2)	(3)	(4)	(5)	(6)	(7)
	DM/ dollar	DM/ dollar (1975 =100)	Wholesale price indices Germany	United States	Real ex- change rate (2/3÷4)	United labor cost Germany	United States
1960	4.170	169.5	64.8	54.3	142.0	—	70
1965	3.994	162.4	69.1	55.2	129.7	59	67
1970	3.647	148.3	73.9	63.1	126.6	70	79
1975	2.460	100.0	100.0	100.0	100.0	100	100
1976	2.518	102.4	103.7	104.6	103.3	99	102
1977	2.332	94.4	106.3	111.0	98.4	102	108
1978	2.009	81.7	107.8	119.7	90.7	106	114
1979	1.833	74.5	113.0	134.7	88.8	108	122
1980	1.818	73.9	121.5	153.6	93.4	117	137
1981	2.260	91.9	130.9	167.5	117.6	122	146
1982	2.427	98.6	138.6	171.1	121.7	127	159
1982							
Oct	2.530	102.8	139.9	171.5	126.0	131	160
Nov	2.555	103.9	139.8	171.8	127.7	131	160
Dec	2.419	98.3	139.5	171.9	121.1	130	161
1983							
Jan	2.388	97.1	139.5	171.6	119.4	127	161
Feb	2.427	98.7	139.4	172.2	121.9	127	161
Mar	2.408	97.9	139.0	171.9	121.1	124	160
Apr	2.439	99.1	139.5	172.0	122.2	127	159
May	2.468	100.3	139.6	172.5	123.9	124	159
June	2.548	103.6	139.6	173.0	128.4	123	158
July	2.588	105.0	139.7	173.5	130.4	127	156
Aug	2.673	108.7	140.6	174.4	134.8	125	155
Sept	2.668	108.5	140.9	174.7	134.5	125	155
Oct	2.602	105.8	141.1	175.2	131.4	—	154
Nov	2.683	109.1	—	174.8	—	—	—

— Not available.

Sources: IMF, International Financial Statistics: column 1 corresponds to line rf, columns 3 and 4 correspond to line 63, columns 10 and 11 correspond to line 65, and columns 13 and 14

TABLE A-2   (*Continued*)

(8) Comparative costs (6/7)	(9) Real exchange rate (2/8)	(10) Wages in manufacturing Germany	(11) Wages in manufacturing United States	(12) Comparative wages (10/11)	(13) Consumer price indices Germany	(14) Consumer price indices United States
—	—	28	47	.596	57.6	55.0
.881	184.4	43	54	.796	65.9	58.6
.886	167.4	63	70	.900	74.2	72.1
1.000	100.0	100	100	1.000	100.0	100.0
.971	105.5	107	108	.991	104.3	105.8
.944	100.0	115	118	.975	108.1	112.7
.930	87.9	120	128	.938	111.1	121.2
.885	83.5	127	139	.914	115.6	134.9
.854	86.5	135	151	.894	122.0	153.1
.836	110.0	143	165	.867	129.2	169.0
.800	123.3	149	176	.847	136.0	179.4
.819	125.6	150	177	.847	137.6	182.4
.819	126.9	150	178	.843	138.0	182.1
.807	121.7	150	180	.833	138.3	181.4
.789	123.1	151	180	.839	138.6	181.9
.789	125.1	151	181	.839	138.7	181.9
.755	129.7	151	181	.839	138.6	182.0
.799	124.1	154	182	.846	138.8	183.2
.780	128.6	154	182	.846	139.5	184.3
.778	133.1	154	182	.846	139.9	184.9
.814	129.0	155	183	.847	140.4	185.7
.806	134.9	155	183	.847	140.9	186.3
.806	134.6	155	184	.842	141.1	187.2
—	—	—	—	—	141.1	187.6
—	—	—	—	—	141.5	—

correspond to line 64. OECD, *Main Economic Indicators:* columns 6 and 7 are taken from country tables on adjusted unit labor costs.

dollar exchange rate (column 2) with the ratio of Japanese to American wholesale prices yields one measure of the "real" exchange rate. From column 5, purchasing power parity seems to be reestablished at the nominal yen/dollar exchange rate prevailing in early 1984. The net depreciation of the dollar from ¥297 in 1975 to about ¥235 to ¥240 now apparently just offsets the higher rate of inflation in the US wholesale price index. The use of consumer price indices would yield a similar result.

Looking at labor costs, however, gives an entirely different impression. The Organization for Economic Cooperation and Development (OECD) provides indices of domestic unit labor costs of producing one real "unit" of manufacturing output. In table A-1, column 6 shows an increase of 12 percent in Japanese unit labor costs from 1975 through 1982, and column 7 shows an increase of 59 percent in the United States. Clearly, the moderate 25 percent nominal appreciation of the yen since 1975 was insufficient to close this gap. The result is the 19.1 percent overvaluation of the dollar's real exchange rate averaged over 1982, as measured in column 9. In 1983, with the nominal exchange rate fluctuating between ¥230 and ¥240 per dollar, the real overvaluation of the dollar against the yen was between 10 percent and 15 percent by this alternative measure. As shown in table 5.1, in 1983 and early 1984 the purchasing power parity exchange rate for equalizing unit labor costs is about ¥210.

However, the calculation of broad unit indices of labor costs is inherently suspect because they contain dissimilar manufactured goods—making cross-country comparisons even more difficult. We need some supporting evidence of a fall in Japanese labor costs relative to the American at existing exchange rates.

Table A-1 shows the pattern of Japanese unit labor costs *rising* relative to those in the United States from 1960 to 1975. Starting from a much lower base, Japanese productivity growth in 1960–75 has been much higher than that of the United States, but it was more than offset by more rapidly rising money wages in Japanese manufacturing. Columns 10 through 12 in table A-1 show how, relative to our 1975 base, wages in Japan more than tripled from 1960 to 1975 compared with those in the United States. This rapid rise caused Japanese unit costs (column 8) to increase from 0.586 of American unit costs in 1960 to 1.000 in 1975.

Prior to 1975, this continual increase in comparative Japanese labor costs was consistent with real exchange market equilibrium. From a limited range of simple goods, Japanese manufacturing evolved toward increasingly sophisticated products. Low-technology goods, such as textiles and toys, were continually phased out as their unit labor costs rose. And we know that output indices tend to underweight quality improvements in high-technology goods. Continual increases in Japanese export prowess in new goods largely offset their increasing costs in old goods.

While more modest since 1975, Japanese productivity growth remained considerably higher than in the United States, where it has been almost nil until 1983. And nobody could doubt that the Japanese capability of developing new export products is as great as ever. But, since 1975, American money wages have grown more than Japanese—in sharp contrast to the record before 1975, as columns 10 to 12 of table A-1 make clear. After exchange rate adjustment, column 9 shows the historically unusual fall in Japanese unit labor costs relative to their American counterparts from 1975 to 1982 *despite* the continual upgrading of Japanese industry from low-technology to high-technology products. The ultracompetitiveness of Japanese manufactured exports, across a wide spectrum of technical sophistication, in American markets in 1982–83 is a manifestation of an undervalued yen.

THE MARK/DOLLAR RATE

Since 1975, price inflation in the United States has been about 23 percent higher than in Germany when comparing wholesale or consumer price indices in table A-2. But the dollar has actually appreciated since 1975 in nominal terms: from DM 2.46 in 1975 to between DM 2.5 and DM 2.6 in late 1982, and as high as DM 2.83 in early February 1984. Consequently, using a real exchange rate calculation based on wholesale prices (column 5, table A-2) the dollar appears overvalued against the mark by about 21.7 percent on average in 1982, and considerably more for some months of 1983 into 1984—closer to 28 or 30 percent—in the neighborhood of DM 2.6.

Similarly, unit labor costs in German manufacturing rose less quickly than in the United States—27 percent vis-à-vis 59 percent—because of higher German productivity growth and relatively restrained wage claims since 1975. The real mark/dollar rate based on unit labor costs (column 9) indicates that the dollar may be overvalued by more than 25 percent in late 1983 and early 1984.

In Japan, yen undervaluation was manifested in higher profit margins as wholesale prices rose. In Germany, by contrast, the undervalued mark is manifested in prices of finished goods well below their American equivalents. Indeed, a profit squeeze and series of bankruptcies and industrial failures in

Europe suggest that profit margins have not been as well maintained as in Japan.

European profit margins are now quite high in export activities that compete against American goods—although they remain quite low domestically. This undervaluation of European currencies as a bloc against the US dollar will allow European industries to continually encroach on world markets for American tradable goods.

One important caveat to the above calculations should be noted. To some extent, apparently higher productivity growth of manufacturing labor in Europe since 1975 is bogus. Real wages have been pushed far too high to secure full employment. Thus the absorption of new labor into productive employment has been slower than in the United States. Moreover, the continual increase in European real wages leads firms to shed labor, and thus apparently increase the productivity of those that remain because capital intensity per man rises. This effect shows up, table A-2 column 6, as a relatively low increase in unit labor costs.

But this European method of achieving productivity growth is neither sustainable nor consistent with full employment. Thus our calculation in column 9 (table A-2) of undervaluation of the German mark seems to be overstated. A 20 percent overvaluation of the dollar is probably a better approximation. After making this correction, the purchasing power parity of the dollar is DM 2.0—as shown in table 5.1.

Appendix B   Interpreting World Money

In equation (5.1) in the text, percentage growth in world money, $\dot{M}^W$, was defined as the weighted sum of individual dollar, mark, and yen growth rates. Though not necessary for specifing an operational rule controlling world money growth, the absolute scale of world money may be of interest to some readers. To move from percentage rates of growth to absolute levels, let us integrate equation (5.1) to obtain:

$$(5.2) \quad \log M^W = .45\log M^{US} + .35\log M^{GE} + .20\log M^{JA} + \log S,$$

where $\log S$ is the constant of integration. But S does have an economic interpretation. It is a scale factor—an unknown and unneeded amalgam of hypothetical or actual exchange rates. To see this more clearly, take the antilog of equation (5.2) to obtain:

$$(5.3) \quad M^W = S(M^{US})^{.45}(M^{GE})^{.35}(M^{JA})^{.20}.$$

If the absolute level of M^W, as defined by equation (5.3), were to be used for any analytical or policy purpose, the relevant exchange rates linking M^{US} to M^{GE} to M^{JA} would have to be specified. For example, suppose we arbitrarily decide to express our monetary index M^W in dollars; then some current or base period, dollar/mark, S^G, and dollar/yen, S^J, exchange rates need to be determined to replace the undefined S in equation (5.3). The "absolute" value of world money in dollars would then be:

$$(5.4) \quad M^W = (M^{US})^{.45}(S^G M^{GE})^{.35}(S^J M^{JA})^{.20}.$$

Fortunately, however, our monetary rule is concerned only with linking the percentage growth rates in M^{US}, M^{GE}, and M^{JA} with fixed weights and not letting aggregate growth be influenced by exchange rates. Hence, we may work from equation (5.1) in the text, and ignore all the exchange rate complications associated with equation (5.2) or (5.3). Other than its simplicity, this methodology is valid in the deeper economic sense that desired world money growth should indeed be independent of exchange rate fluctuations. Otherwise, our rule would not provide an independent and unambiguous monetary anchor for the world price level.

Appendix C   Statistical Appendix

TABLE C-1   **The dollar exchange rate and growth in US nominal GNP, 1958–83 (money growth by calendar year)**

$\dot{Y}^{US}$	C	$\dot{M}^{US}$	$\dot{M}^{US}_{-1}$	$\dot{M}^{US}_{-2}$	$\bar{R}^2$	SE	DW	Period
4.05 (3.96)	−0.02 (−0.07)	0.96 (3.98)	−0.11 (0.38)		0.58	1.65	2.64	1958–69
4.01 (4.69)		0.96 (4.38)	−0.12 (−0.46)		0.63	1.56	2.62	1958–69
3.92 (0.86)	1.68 (2.62)	−0.77 (−1.19)			0.33	2.07	1.22	1972–82
1.60 (0.28)	1.93 (2.55)	−1.05 (−1.34)	0.40 (0.69)		0.28	2.50	1.05	1972–82
8.56 (1.51)	0.26 (0.60)	−0.10 (−0.15)			−0.19	2.72	1.35	1972–83[a]

$\dot{Y}^{US}$	C	$\dot{M}^{US}$	$\dot{M}^{US}_{-1}$	$\dot{E}$	$\dot{E}_{-1}$	$\bar{R}^2$	SE	DW	Period
6.68 (3.11)	1.91 (6.27)	−1.45 (−4.73)	−0.02 (−0.30)	−0.29 (−4.99)		0.87	0.91	1.49	1972–82
6.49 (3.38)	1.95 (7.28)	−1.45 (−5.10)		−0.30 (−6.35)		0.89	0.85	1.62	1972–82
10.30 (2.97)	0.98 (2.74)	−1.10 (−2.02)		−0.35 (−3.94)		0.55	1.68	1.11	1972–83[a]

Notes: Results of fitting equations (4.1 and 4.2). T-statistics for regression coefficients are in parentheses. *SE* denotes the standard regression error, and *DW* is the Durbin Watson statistic. Observations on money and GNP are percentage changes in annual averages. All regressions are ordinary least squares. $\dot{E}$ is concurrent percentage change in dollar exchange rate, and $\dot{E}_{-1}$ is lagged one calendar year (see bottom of figure 1.1). Similarly, percentage growth in nominal GNP is denoted by $\dot{Y}^{US}$, and percentage growth in M1 is denoted by $\dot{M}^{US}$

Source: US GNP taken from IMF, *International Financial Statistics,* see table 4.5. M1 data are from the Federal Reserve Bank of St. Louis, see table 4.2

a. Preliminary data.

TABLE C-2   **The dollar exchange rate and growth in US nominal GNP, 1958–83 (money growth lagged 6 and 18 months)**

$\dot{Y}^{US}$	C	$\dot{M}^{US}_{-6m}$	$\dot{M}^{US}_{-18m}$	$\dot{E}$	$\dot{E}_{-1}$	$\bar{R}^2$	SE	DW	Period
	3.80	1.22	−0.35			0.80	1.13	1.37	1958–69
	(6.18)	(6.53)	(−1.73)						
	8.69	1.59	−1.37			0.50	1.78	1.55	1972–82
	(2.51)	(3.20)	(−2.73)						
	9.85	0.70	−0.72			0.02	2.48	1.05	1972–83[a]
	(2.05)	(1.25)	(−1.14)						
	13.25	1.34	−1.84	0.05	−0.28	0.85	0.98	2.03	1972–82
	(6.09)	(4.24)	(4.24)	(0.86)	(−4.33)				
	13.37	1.22	−1.74		−0.26	0.86	0.96	2.20	1972–82
	(6.27)	(4.39)	(−6.16)		(−4.54)				
	15.04	0.83	−1.62		−0.33	0.78	1.18	1.84	1972–83[a]
	(6.10)	(3.08)	(−4.74)		(−5.61)				

Notes: See table C-1. $\dot{M}^{US}_{-6m}$ is annual percentage growth in American M1 lagged 6 months, and $\dot{M}^{US}_{-18m}$ is lagged 18 months. $\dot{E}$ is concurrent percentage change in dollar exchange rate, and $\dot{E}_{-1}$ is lagged one year (see bottom of figure 1.1).
Source: US GNP taken from IMF, *International Financial Statistics,* see table 4.5. M1 data are taken from the Federal Reserve Bank of St. Louis, see table 4.2.
a. Preliminary data.

TABLE C-3   **The dollar exchange rate and American tradable goods prices, 1972–82**

$\dot{P}^{US}$	C	$\dot{M}^{US}_{-6m}$	$\dot{M}^{US}_{-18m}$	$\dot{E}$	$\dot{E}_{-1}$	$\dot{E}_{-2}$	SE	$\overline{R}^2$	DW
	-4.96	-0.63	2.72				4.29	0.26	1.05
	(-0.59)	(-0.53)	(2.25)						
	5.38	-1.51	1.99	-0.03	-0.54		3.05	0.62	2.00
	(0.79)	(-1.53)	(2.03)	(-0.18)	(-2.68)				
	5.30	-1.43	1.92		-0.56		2.83	0.68	2.09
	(0.84)	(-1.74)	(2.29)		(-3.36)				
	4.62	-0.51	0.99		-0.50	-0.42	2.52	0.74	1.37
	(0.82)	(-0.55)	(1.07)		(-3.33)	(-1.69)			

$\dot{P}^{US}$	C	$\dot{M}^{US}_{-1}$	$\dot{M}^{US}_{-2}$	$\dot{E}$	$\dot{E}_{-1}$	$\dot{E}_{-2}$	SE	$\overline{R}^2$	DW
	-10.57	0.96	2.11				3.95	0.37	0.97
	(-1.30)	(0.82)	(2.24)						
	-3.74	0.11	1.86	-0.05	-0.45		2.80	0.68	2.33
	(-0.59)	(0.12)	(2.33)	(-0.29)	(-2.44)				
	-3.50	0.18	1.74		-0.48		2.61	0.73	2.29
	(0.61)	(0.23)	(2.76)		(-3.37)				
	-1.66	0.67	0.81		-0.45	-0.43	2.14	0.82	1.73
	(-0.35)	(0.95)	(1.20)		(-3.82)	(-2.10)			

Notes: See table C-1. $\dot{M}^{US}$ is annual percentage growth in American M1 based on calendar years (table 4.2). $\dot{M}^{US}_{-1}$ is lagged one calendar year, and $\dot{M}^{US}_{-2}$ is lagged two calendar years. $\dot{M}^{US}_{-6m}$ is annual growth in American M1 lagged 6 months, and $\dot{M}^{US}_{-18m}$ is lagged 18 months. $\dot{E}_{-1}$ and $\dot{E}_{-2}$ are percentage rates of change in the dollar exchange rate lagged by one and two calendar years respectively (see bottom of figure 1.1). $\dot{P}^{US}$ is the annual percentage change in the US wholesale price index.

Sources: See table C-5. Results from fitting equation (4.4).

TABLE C-4   **The dollar exchange rate and price inflation in American tradable goods, 1972–83**[a]

$\dot{P}^{US}$	C	$\dot{M}^{US}_{-6m}$	$\dot{M}^{US}_{-18m}$	$\dot{E}$	$\dot{E}_{-1}$	$\dot{E}_{-2}$	SE	$\bar{R}^2$	DW
	−4.29	−1.14	3.10				4.18	0.37	1.39
	(−0.53)	(−1.21)	(2.90)						
	3.30	−0.95	1.78	0.03	−0.48		3.00	0.68	2.04
	(0.53)	(−1.29)	(1.91)	(0.02)	(−2.58)				
	3.30	−0.96	1.78		−0.48		2.81	0.72	2.04
	(0.56)	(−1.51)	(2.19)		(3.45)				
	2.01	−0.13	1.09		−0.40	−0.29	2.76	0.73	1.57
	(0.34)	(−0.13)	(1.08)		(−2.68)	(−1.12)			

$\dot{P}^{US}$	C	$\dot{M}^{US}_{-1}$	$\dot{M}^{US}_{-2}$	$\dot{E}$	$\dot{E}_{-1}$	$\dot{E}_{-2}$	SE	$\bar{R}^2$	DW
	−10.60	1.26	1.68				4.76	0.18	0.64
	(−1.08)	(0.90)	(1.51)						
	−2.41	0.11	1.61	−0.01	−0.55		2.78	0.72	2.40
	(−0.40)	(0.12)	(2.14)	(−0.08)	(−3.66)				
	−2.36	0.13	1.58		−0.56		2.60	0.76	2.40
	(−0.42)	(0.16)	(2.60)		(−4.71)				
	−2.72	0.55	1.16		−0.43	−0.30	2.09	0.84	1.90
	(−0.60)	(0.82)	(2.24)		(−3.82)	(−2.32)			

Notes: See table C-3.
Source: See table C-5. Results from fitting equation (4.4).
a. The 1983 data used in the regressions are preliminary.

TABLE C-5   **Price inflation in tradable goods and growth in US and world money, 1958–83**

$\dot{P}^{US}$ C	$\dot{M}^{US}$	$\dot{M}^{US}_{-1}$	$\dot{M}^{US}_{-2}$	$\bar{R}^2$	SE	DW	Period
−0.94 (−1.35)	0.32 (−1.73)	0.21 (1.29)	0.13 (0.64)	0.43	1.09	1.87	1958–69
−0.83 (−1.28)	0.37 (2.18)	0.23 (1.49)		0.47	1.12	1.99	1958–69
3.65 (0.34)	−1.39 (−1.00)	1.79 (1.25)	1.60 (1.50)	0.37	3.95	1.11	1972–82
−10.57 (−1.30)		0.96 (0.82)	*2.11* (2.24)	0.37	3.95	0.99	1972–82
−1.72 (−0.21)	−1.77 (−2.60)	−2.04 (1.80)	1.43 (1.63)	0.50	3.72	1.72	1972–83[a]

$\dot{P}^{US}$ C	$\dot{M}^{W}$	$\dot{M}^{W}_{-1}$	$\dot{M}^{W}_{-2}$	$\dot{E}_{-1}$	$\bar{R}^2$	SE	DW	Period
−3.15 (−0.92)	0.45 (1.04)	0.21 (0.66)	0.05 (0.15)		−0.14	1.59	1.20	1958–69
−4.98 (−1.18)	−1.12 (−2.63)	1.14 (2.83)	1.45 (4.68)		0.82	2.10	2.62	1972–82
4.56 (1.16)	−1.72 (−3.13)	0.99 (1.56)	0.75 (1.56)	−0.37 (−3.36)	0.93	1.33	2.03	1972–82

Notes: See table C-3 and table C-1. Results from fitting equation (4.3) $\dot{M}^{W}$ denotes annual percentage growth in "world" money (taken from table 4.1) for 11 industrial countries. $\dot{P}^{US}$ denotes annual percentage growth in the American wholesale price index.
Source: M1 data from Federal Reserve Bank of St. Louis, see table 4.1. Data on wholesale prices from IMF, *International Financial Statistics,* line 63, see table 4.4.
a. Preliminary data.

References

Ambler, Steven. September 1983. "On Calculating Net Foreign Asset Positions." Unpublished paper. Stanford, Calif.: Stanford University. Processed.

———. January 1984. "The Contractionary Effects of a Temporary Fiscal Expansion." Unpublished paper. Stanford, Calif.: Stanford University. Processed.

Bergsten, C. Fred. 23 September 1983. "Currency Crisis." *The New York Times*.

Bergsten, C. Fred, and John Williamson. 1984. *The Multiple Reserve Currency System*. Washington: Institute for International Economics. Forthcoming.

Bernholz, Peter. July 1982. *Flexible Exchange Rates in Historical Perspective*. Studies in International Finance No. 49. Princeton, N.J.: International Finance Section.

Brittan, Samuel. 12 July 1982. "A New Policy for the Fed." *Financial Times*.

Burgstaller, André. October 1983. "Contractionary Effects of an Anticipated Fiscal Stimulus in the Flexible Exchange-Rate Economy." Unpublished paper. New York: Columbia University. Processed.

Cline, William R. September 1983. *International Debt and the Stability of the World Economy*. POLICY ANALYSES IN INTERNATIONAL ECONOMICS 4. Washington: Institute for International Economics.

Dornbusch, Rudiger. December 1976. "Expectations and Exchange Rate Dynamics." *Journal of Political Economy*, vol. 84, no. 6.

———. September 1982. "Equilibrium and Disequilibrium Exchange Rates." National Bureau of Economic Research (NBER) Working Paper no. 983. Cambridge, Mass.: NBER. Processed.

———. March 1983. "Flexible Exchange Rates and Interdependence." International Monetary Fund (IMF) *Staff Papers*, vol. 30, no. 1. Washington.

Federal Reserve Bank of St. Louis. January 1984. "International Economic Conditions." St. Louis.

Frenkel, Jacob, and Michael L. Mussa. May 1980. "The Efficiency of the Foreign Exchange Market and Measures of Turbulence." *American Economic Review, Papers and Proceedings*, vol. 70, no. 2.

Friedman, Milton. 1953. "The Case for Flexible Exchange Rates." In *Essays in Positive Economics*. Chicago: University of Chicago Press.

Friedman, Milton. March 1968. "The Role of Monetary Policy." *American Economic Review*, vol. 58, no. 1.

Haberler, Gottfried. 1949. "The Market for Foreign Exchange and the Stability of the Balance of Payments: A Theoretical Analysis." *Kyklos*, vol. 3.

Henderson, Dale W. February 1982. "The Role of Intervention Policy in Open Economy Financial Policy: A Macroeconomic Perspective." International Finance Discussion Paper No. 202. Washington: Board of Governors of the Federal Reserve System. Processed.

International Monetary Fund (IMF). 1983. *International Financial Statistics Yearbook*. Washington.

————. February 1984. *International Financial Statistics*. Washington.

Johnson, Harry G. 1972. "The Case for Flexible Exchange Rates, 1969." In *Further Essays in Monetary Economics*. Cambridge, Mass.: Harvard University Press.

Karaken, J., and N. Wallace. May 1981. "On the Indeterminacy of Equilibrium Exchange Rates." *Quarterly Journal of Economics*, vol. 96, no. 2.

Kenen, Peter B. 1983. "The Role of the Dollar as an International Currency." *Occasional Papers* No. 13. New York: Group of Thirty.

Machlup, Fritz. 1972. *The Alignment of Foreign Exchange Rates*. New York: Praeger.

MaGee, Stephen P. 1973. "Currency Contracts, Pass-Through and Devaluation." *Brookings Papers in Economic Activity*, no. 1.

McKinnon, Ronald I. September 1963. "Optimum Currency Areas." *American Economic Review*, vol. 53, no. 4.

————. October 1974. *A New Tripartite Monetary Agreement or a Limping Dollar Standard?* Essays in International Finance No. 106. Princeton, N.J.: International Finance Section.

————. 1979. *Money in International Exchange: The Convertible Currency System*. New York: Oxford University Press.

————. 1981. "Exchange-Rate Instability, Trade Imbalances, and Monetary Policies in Japan, Europe, and the United States." In *Issues in International Economics*, Peter Oppenheimer, ed. Oxford International Symposia, vol. 5. Boston: Routledge & Kegan Paul.

————. June 1981. "The Exchange Rate and Macroeconomic Policy: Changing Postwar Perceptions." *Journal of Economic Literature*, vol. 19, no. 2.

————. June 1982. "Currency Substitution and Instability in the World Dollar Standard." *American Economic Review*, vol. 72, no. 30.

————. 1983. "The J-Curve, Stabilizing Speculation, and Capital Constraints on Foreign Exchange Dealers." In *Exchange Rate and Trade Instability: Causes, Consequences, and Remedies*, David Bigman and Teizo Taya, eds. Cambridge, Mass.: Ballinger Publishing Co.

————. July 1983. "Why Floating Exchange Rates Fail." Hoover Institution Working Papers in Economics. Stanford, Calif.: Stanford University. Processed.

McKinnon, Ronald I., and Kong-Yam Tan. July 1983. "The Dollar Exchange Rate as a Monetary Indicator: Reply to Radcliffe, Warga and Willett." Stanford, Calif.: Stanford University. Processed.

Meade, J.E. September 1955. "The Case for Variable Exchange Rates." *Three Banks Review*, vol. 27.

Michaely, Michael. 1971. *The Responsiveness of Demand Policies to Balance of Payments*. New York: NBER, Columbia University Press.

Modigliani, Franco. 1973. "International Capital Movements, Fixed Parities, and Monetary and Fiscal Policies." In *Development and Planning: Essays in Honour of Paul Rosenstein Rodan*, Jagdish N. Bhagwati and Richard S. Eckaus, eds. Cambridge, Mass.: MIT Press.

Mundell, Robert A. September 1961. "A Theory of Optimum Currency Areas." *American Economic Review*, vol. 51, no. 4.

———. 1969. "The Redundancy Problem and the Price Level." In *Monetary Problems of the International Economy*, Robert A. Mundell and Alexander K. Swoboda, eds. Chicago: University of Chicago Press.

Organization for Economic Cooperation and Development (OECD). September 1983. *Main Economic Indicators*. Paris: OECD Department of Economics and Statistics.

Radcliffe, Christopher, Arthur Warga, and Thomas Willett. March 1983a. "Currency Substitution and Instability in the World Dollar Standard: Comment." Unpublished paper. Claremont, Calif.: Claremont University. Processed.

———. 1983b. "Currency Substitution and Instability in the World Dollar Standard: Further Comments." Claremont Working Papers. Claremont, Calif.: Claremont University. Processed.

Swoboda, Alexander K. September 1978. "Gold, Dollars, Euro-Dollars, and the World Money Stock Under Fixed Exchange Rates." *American Economic Review*, vol. 68.

Tan, Kong-Yam. 1984. "Flexible Exchange Rates and Interdependence: Empirical Implications for US Monetary Policy." Ph.D. diss. Stanford, Calif.: Stanford University.

Tobin, James. 1982. "The State of Exchange Rate Theory: Some Skeptical Observations." In *The International Monetary System Under Flexible Exchange Rates*, Richard N. Cooper, Peter B. Kenen, Jorge Braga de Macedo, and Jacques van Ypersele, eds. Cambridge, Mass.: Ballinger Publishing Company.

Triffin, Robert. 1960. *Gold and the Dollar Crisis*. New Haven, Conn.: Yale University Press.

Wall Street Journal. 2 August 1983. "US, Germany and Japan Intervene To Stabilize Exchange Markets."

Williamson, John. September 1983a. *The Exchange Rate System*. POLICY ANALYSES IN INTERNATIONAL ECONOMICS 5. Washington: Institute for International Economics.

———. 1983b. "Keynes and the International Economic Order." Paper presented to a conference sponsored by the Royal Economic Society, King's College, and the University of Cambridge Faculty of Economics and Politics on "The Relevance of Keynes's Economics Today," to celebrate the centennial of the birth of John Maynard Keynes. July 15–16, 1983. King's College, Cambridge, England. Processed.

Witteveen, H.J. November 1982. "Where Do We Go From Here?" *The Banker*, vol. 132, no. 681.

Order from your local bookseller, or from
The MIT Press, 28 Carleton Street, Cambridge, Mass. 02142

ORDER INFORMATION

- Standing orders for all publications or for POLICY ANALYSES only are invited from companies, institutions, and libraries in the United States and Canada. Write MIT Press for information.
- Orders from individuals must be accompanied by payment in US dollars, credit card number, or request for a proforma invoice.
- Prices outside the United States and Canada are slightly higher. Write MIT Press for a proforma invoice.

Order	Book code	Unit price	Number of copies	Total
Standing order for				
☐ All publications, POLICY ANALYSES and hardcover books				
☐ All POLICY ANALYSES				
☐ All past publications, POLICY ANALYSES and hardcover books	—	$122.00	_____	_____
☐ All past POLICY ANALYSES only	—	48.00	_____	_____

POLICY ANALYSES IN INTERNATIONAL ECONOMICS

Published

1. *The Lending Policies of the International Monetary Fund* John Williamson August 1982	WILPP	6.00	_____	_____
2. *"Reciprocity": A New Approach to World Trade Policy?* William R. Cline September 1982	CLIRP	6.00	_____	_____
3. *Trade Policy in the 1980s* C. Fred Bergsten and William R. Cline November 1982	BERTP	6.00	_____	_____
4. *International Debt and the Stability of the World Economy* William R. Cline September 1983	CLIIP	6.00	_____	_____
5. *The Exchange Rate System* John Williamson September 1983	WILEP	6.00	_____	_____
6. *Economic Sanctions in Support of Foreign Policy Goals* Gary Clyde Hufbauer and Jeffrey J. Schott October 1983	HUFEP	6.00	_____	_____
7. *A New SDR Allocation?* John Williamson March 1984	WILNP	6.00	_____	_____
8. *An International Standard for Monetary Stabilization* Ronald I. McKinnon March 1984	MCKNP	6.00	_____	_____

Forthcoming

The Multiple Reserve Currency System C. Fred Bergsten and John Williamson Summer 1984	BERMP	6.00	_____	_____
Second-Best Responses to Currency Misalignments Stephen Marris Summer 1984	MARSP	6.00	_____	_____
Reforming Trade Adjustment Policy Gary Clyde Hufbauer and Howard F. Rosen Winter 1984–85	HUFRP	6.00	_____	_____
Financial Intermediation Beyond the Debt Crisis John Williamson Summer 1984	WILFP	6.00	_____	_____
Toward Cartelization of World Steel Trade? William R. Cline Summer 1984	CLITP	6.00	_____	_____
International Trade in Automobiles: Liberalization or Further Restraint? William R. Cline Fall 1984	CLINP	6.00	_____	_____
New International Arrangements for Foreign Direct Investment C. Fred Bergsten and Jeffrey J. Schott Fall 1984	BERAP	6.00	_____	_____
Another Multi-Fiber Arrangement? William R. Cline Winter 1984–85	CLIAP	6.00	_____	_____

BOOKS
Published

IMF Conditionality John Williamson, ed. May 1983	WILIH	30.00	_____	_____
Trade Policy in the 1980s William R. Cline, ed. November 1983	CLITH	35.00		

Forthcoming

Subsidies in International Trade Gary Clyde Hufbauer and Joanna Shelton Erb Spring 1984	HUFSH	30.00	_____	_____
International Debt: Systemic Risk and Policy Response William R. Cline April 1984	CLIIH	20.00	_____	_____
Economic Sanctions Reconsidered: History and Current Policy Gary Clyde Hufbauer and Jeffrey J. Schott Spring 1984	HUFEH	35.00	_____	_____
Domestic Adjustment and International Trade Gary Clyde Hufbauer and Howard F. Rosen Winter 1984–85	HUFDH	25.00	_____	_____

Order	Book code	Unit price	Number of copies	Total
International Coordination of National Economic Policies Stephen Marris Winter 1984–85	MAROH	6.00	_____	_____
Trade Controls in Three Industries: The Automobile, Steel, and Textile Cases William R. Cline Winter 1984–85	CLICH	25.00	_____	_____

Special Reports

Promoting World Recovery: A Statement on Global Economic Strategy by Twenty-six Economists from Fourteen Countries December 1982	TWEPP	3.00	_____	_____
Prospects for Adjustment in Argentina, Brazil, and Mexico: Responding to the Debt Crisis John Williamson, ed. June 1983	WILAP	6.00	_____	_____

SUBTOTAL   US$ _____

POSTAGE

Domestic: Book rate $1.50 each hardcover; $0.75 each paper. First class $3.50 each hardcover; $2.50 each paper.

Foreign: Surface $0.75 each paper; $1.75 each hardcover. Airmail $8.00 each hardcover; $3.00 each paper.

Postage _____

TOTAL US$ _____

PAYMENT
☐ Purchase order attached. ☐ Check enclosed (drawn to The MIT Press). Charge to
☐ MasterCard
☐ VISA, number _____

(Minimum credit card order $10.00)   Expiration date _____

Ship to

NAME _____

    Please print   First   Middle   Last

AFFILIATION _____

ADDRESS _____ CITY _____

STATE OR PROVINCE _____ POSTAL CODE _____ COUNTRY _____

Offer expires May 31, 1984

Other Institute Publications
POLICY ANALYSES IN INTERNATIONAL ECONOMICS

Forthcoming

Second-Best Responses to Currency Misalignments   Stephen Marris
Currency misalignments have led to resort to, and proposals for, trade restrictions, border taxes, capital controls, interest equalization taxes, "compensatory finance," and a range of other "second-best" devices. The study will assess these alternatives and their utility under differing circumstances.   Summer 1984.

The Multiple Reserve Currency System   C. Fred Bergsten and John Williamson
A study of the rapidly growing use of several national currencies (especially the DM and yen) as international reserve assets and its implications for exchange rate stability and the world's financial system.   Summer 1984.

Published

7   *A New SDR Allocation?*   John Williamson
An assessment of the case for a new allocation of special drawing rights in the light of the debt crisis and misalignment of major exchange rates. Describes the agreed criteria governing allocations, presents the statistics relevant to those criteria, and appraises the economic arguments concerning the timeliness and scale of a new allocation.   March 1984.

Books

Forthcoming

International Debt: Systemic Risk and Policy Response   William R. Cline
A study of the origins of the international debt problem and recent trends that have intensified it, the financial system's vulnerability, and the adequacy of bank regulation and of central bank "lender-of-last-resort facilities." Includes detailed examination of selected major countries and statistical "early warning indicators" of the need for debt reschedulings.   April 1984.

Subsidies in International Trade   Gary Clyde Hufbauer and Joanna Shelton Erb
An explanation and analysis of concepts underlying the subsidy problem and the most important issues it raises for international economic policy. Domestic subsidies are defined and related to international trade, and proposals are made for dealing with them constructively. Changes in the existing international regime and domestic legal structure are recommended to limit the adverse economic and political effects of subsidy practices.   Spring 1984.

Economic Sanctions Reconsidered: History and Current Policy   Gary Clyde Hufbauer and Jeffrey J. Schott, assisted by Kimberly Ann Elliott
An analysis of more than one hundred cases of economic sanctions imposed in pursuit of national foreign policy goals. Develops a detailed methodology for judging the success of such efforts and for assessing the economic effects on the imposing country as well as the target country and derives "nine commandments" to guide sanctions decisions in the future.   Spring 1984.

Published

IMF Conditionality   John Williamson, editor
Twenty-one papers analyzing the role of the Fund in the financing and adjustment of balance of payments problems, the criteria for judging Fund lending, twelve country studies of Fund performance, and a series of conclusions and policy implications. Asks whether Fund conditions have been appropriate to different countries' circumstances and at different times.   May 1983.

Distributed by MIT Press
Cambridge, Massachusetts, and London, England
ISSN 0733-1738
ISBN 0-262-63093-1
MCKNP

DATE DUE

MAR 5 - 1987	MAR 2 0 1994		
	MAR 2 2 199		
SEP 2 2 1988	AUG 1 4 1995		
OCT 2 0 1988	AUG 1 5 199		
NOV 2 8 1988			
DEC 2 2 1988	APR 1 8 2002		
FEB 0 9 1989	MAY 0 9 2002		
MAR 2 0 1989			
APR 2 0 1989			
DEC 0 9 1991			
JAN 1 5 1992			
FEB 1 2 1992			
MAR 1 1 1992			
APR 0 8 1992			
APR 0 7 1992			
MAY 2 4 1993			
MAY 1 2 1993			PRINTED IN U.S.A

GAYLORD